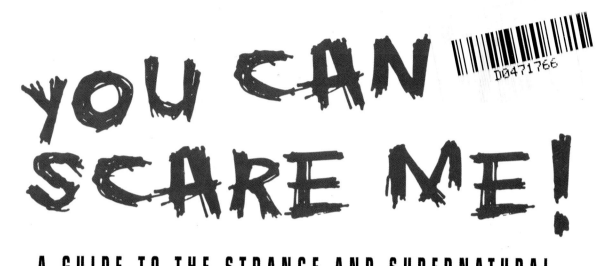

YOU CAN SCARE ME!

A GUIDE TO THE STRANGE AND SUPERNATURAL

ticktock

First published in North America in 2010 by *ticktock* Media Ltd.,
The Old Sawmill, 103 Goods Station Road, Tunbridge Wells, Kent TN1 2DP, U.K.

ISBN: 978-1-84696-202-8

Printed in China
9 8 7 6 5 4 3 2 1

Picture credits (t=top; b=bottom; c=center; l=left; r=right; OFC=outside front cover; OBC=outside back cover):
AKG: 8–9b, 9tr, 11b, 14 (main), 15t, 17br, 18t, 34–35b, 34–35c, 35cr, 35tr, 36–37 (main), 37cl, 37tl, 40tl, 41r, 42tr, 42–43c, 43br, 46b, 46c, 48cl, 50c, 57c, 58–59c, 60c, 64tl, 68cb, 70–71b, 72tl, 73br, 79c, 82tl, 123cr. Allsport: 10b. British Museum: 65t. Alastair Carew-Cox: 125cr. J. Allan Cash: 29r. CFCL: 38l. Colorific: 64–65. Corbis: 6tl, 11 (main), 12–13c, 17tr, 19b, 22 (main), 22br, 23b, 26tl, 30bl, 30–31 (main), 31tr, 39tr, 41cl, 49tr, 58c, 64–65b, 66bl, 74–75b, 76bl, 84cl, 84tl, 84–85c, 104bl, 106b, 118–119 (main). Corbis Royalty Free Images: 108–109. Et Archive: 52–53t, 70–71t. Fortean Picture Library: 2, 8–9c, 12t, 13r, 15cl, 16br, 19c, 20tl, 20c, 20–21b, 21 (main), 23tr, 24 (main), 24–25t, 25tr, 30tl, 32b, 36tl, 40–41c, 50–51bc, 50tl, 51c, 51(main), 54c, 54b, 55tr, 57tr, 57bc, 59tr, 60b, 62 (main), 62–63t, 63b, 63tr, 66–67b, 68l, 68–69ct, 69bl, 70c, 70–71c, 72–73c, 75tr, 80bl, 80–81b, 84b, 85b, 84–85t, 86tr, 87tr, 88b, 88–89c, 89br, 89tr, 90–91cb, 92b, 92c, 93bl, 94–95b, 95tr, 96bl, 96–97b, 97br, 98tl, 99c, 98–99b, 98–99t, 100c, 100tl, 100–101b, 100–101t, 101br, 105tl, 106–107c, 109tr, 109bl, 110tl, 110cl, 111tl, 111cr, 111cl, 112b, 113b, 114tr, 118bl, 121b, 122tl, 124–125t. FPG International; 112–113t. Gamma: 71t. Geoscience: 74bl. Giraudon: 124tl. Groomwatch: 104t. Image Bank: 16t, 32tl. Images: 24–25c, 33 (main), 117r. Images CWP: 43tr, 52tl, 58–59t, 76tl, 90–91t. Image Select: 6b, 16–17c, 22b, 31br, 60–61b, 63c, 67tr, 72bl, 74–75t, 76c, 83tr, 86b, 123t. iStock: OBC, 107r. Kobal: 96–97t. Mary Evans Picture Library: 50–51c, 90cl, 92–93c, 93cr, 99c, 107bl, 110cr, 110br, 111br, 112bl, 115tr. Pictor: 118c, 119tr. Planet Earth Pictures: 27r, 48tl, 48–49br, 52–53c, 121tc. Plymouth City Museum & Art Gallery: 19t. Rex Features: 55tl, 56, 56tr, 56–57c, 120bc. Ronald Grant Archive: 18 (main). Ann Ronan @ Image Select: 4b, 8tl, 15bl, 20l, 23cr, 26b, 27b, 27tr, 39c, 44c, 44cr, 45, 50tl, 52bl, 53cr, 61tr, 66tl, 87c, 91b, 125br. Science Photo Library: 3, 4–5tc, 32tr, 82bl, 82–83c, 86tl, 90tl, 94c, 94–95t, 95cr, 102cb, 102–103cb, 102tl, 102ct, 103, 112tl, 114l, 120tl. Spectrum Colour Library: 8bl, 15br, 118tl. Shutterstock: OFC, 1, 29tr. Telegraph Colour Library: 46–47r, 46tl, 48c, 48–49tc, 54tl, 55 (main), 66c, 116–117c, 120cr, 120–121tc. The Kobal Collection: 27 (main), 34tl, 39bl, 44tl, 44b, 104bl, 106tl, 114c, 114–115. Tony Stone Images: 6–7c, 7 (main), 10tl, 12–13 (main), 25b, 28b, 28t, 28–29 (main), 29br, 64bl, 76–77c, 77tr, 78, 80c, 80tl, 83c, 87 (main), 104–105c, 117cb, 122–123 (main). Werner Forman: 40b, 73tr

The unexplainable mysteries in life intrigue a large number of us. Is this because there is something irresistible about the things for which we have no answer? Or is it the mere suggestion that there might be life beyond our earthly sphere that starts our blood racing? Despite the fact that all these paranormal phenomena are unable to be explained by scientists, a lot of evidence has been gathered to support the claims of those who believe they have witnessed or experienced something otherworldly.

INTRODUCTION

GHOSTS , MONSTERS, & THE SUPERNATURAL

Unidentified flying objects; monsters on land and in the sea; ghosts and werewolves; witches and warlocks—do any of these things really exist? What about people who claim they have received a message from beyond the grave? How about those who believe they have had accurate visions of the future? This book takes you past the hype and shows you real case studies to help you make up your own mind.

SUPERNATURAL IN LITERATURE

A lot has been written about the supernatural world. One of the earliest spooky novels was Bram Stoker's *Dracula*. Ghosts often featured in Shakespeare plays, and novels about beings from other planets are called science fiction. Read about why these subjects have never ceased to delight audiences through the ages.

SCIENCE OF THE PARANORMAL/GHOST BUSTING

The scientific study of unexplainable phenomena is known as parapsychology. *Paranormal* describes any unusual experience that we don't have an explanation for based on our understanding of life on Earth. Paranormal experiences generally seem strange, unbelievable, or unnatural to human beings. Find out about the cutting-edge science used to investigate the unexplained.

FAKES & FRAUDS

For the number of people who have truly observed otherwoldly phenomena, there are just as many stories that turn out to be false. You'll be surprised at the lengths some people will go to make a profit! From dubious photos of UFOs over cityscapes to supposed sea-serpent sightings—make up your own mind about the believability of some of the amazing sights many have witnessed.

CULTURES & THE UNEXPLAINED

Many cultures and religions believe in life beyond this world. Find out all about the otherworldly beliefs of cultures such as Buddhists, shamans, and the ancient Egyptians. Despite many differences in their beliefs, there is clearly something about the unexplained that fascinates—just as much as it baffles—most of us.

WHAT IS A GHOST?

Nobody really knows what a ghost is. Despite the long history of recorded sightings, no basic facts have ever been agreed. Modern researchers continue to investigate the subject, but until more is known, the question of whether or not ghosts exist largely remains a matter of faith. Perhaps the most persistent belief is that ghosts are spirits of the dead. This inevitably links the subject with larger issues of religious belief, cultural superstitions, and scientific theory. Whatever our views, the numerous accounts of extraordinary ghostly sightings and events make this fascinating phenomenon difficult to ignore. Why are there reports of ghosts all around the world and what truth lies behind these strange sightings?

TRICKS & PRANKS

Many photographs of ghosts have proven to be fakes. Ghostly pictures were popular at the end of the 1800s when photography was a new technology. The easiest photographic trick is that of double exposure. This occurs when two separate shots are taken on the same piece of film, resulting in one image being superimposed over another.

PERCEPTIONS

The image of a ghost that comes to mind for most people is a pathetic figure clothed in a white gown, rattling chains and perhaps dragging a ball and manacle behind it. In reality, such an obvious manifestation is rare. Most ghosts seem to appear only once, usually at the moment of their death, and never return to haunt their former home. Many people who claim to have seen a ghost report the experience as a positive and uplifting one. They feel fear only as the ghost begins to materialize.

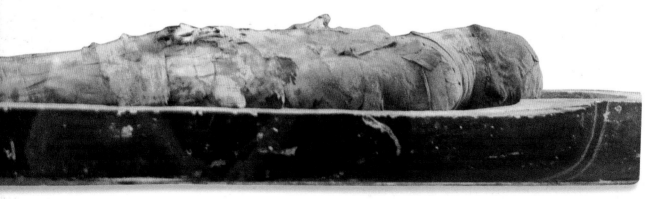

THE AFTERLIFE

Throughout history, most cultures have believed in some form of afterlife. The ancient Egyptians made elaborate preparations for the journey into the afterlife by mummifying and preserving a body after death. The Christian Church promises resurrection of the human soul after death. Ghosts are sometimes thought to be souls or spirits trapped on Earth, unable to pass over to the spiritual plane.

FANTASTIC LIGHTS

Some ghosts may be attributable to natural phenomena. In the past, fantastic lights such as the aurora borealis around the North Pole could have been mistaken for spiritual visitations. A common phenomenon known as will-o'-the-wisp has often been mistaken for ghosts. For centuries, these mysterious pale lights have been seen hovering over marshland. Rather than spirits of the dead, they are the spontaneous combustion of marsh gases.

WHAT IS A MONSTER?

PRIMAL FOREST

Forests can be dark, forbidding places, home to unknown creatures and where it's easy to get lost. For our ancestors, who lived before the days of convenient paths and rest stops, the forest hid enemy attackers and savage predators. Perhaps worst of all was the fear of having an accident and never being found by friends or relatives. Those who wander off the beaten track do so at their peril. "Whatever you do," say wise adults in fairy tales, "don't go into the forest." On the way to her granny's house, Little Red Riding Hood forgot to heed her mother's warning and almost became a wicked wolf's dinner.

Why do we feel the need to be afraid? Monsters are borne out of the dark, out of the unknown, out of the things that human beings don't fully understand. Our ancestors' fears were often justified, and deep in all our souls there still lives a cave dweller, ever fearful of wild animals, ever worried about where the next meal will come from, ever terrified of the dark, thunder, lightning, loneliness, and desertion. Such instinctive fears make us all too willing to believe in monsters. Even today, many people continue to be afraid of the dark because it represents the unknown. With the lights off, our eyes fail us, and our other senses can become confused or even desert us. The human mind fills in gaps, jumps to conclusions, and often creates monsters out of nothing but its own fears.

TOOTH & CLAW

This cat is displaying its fangs because it is scared or angry, but the message it sends to the viewer is that it is not a creature to be underestimated. Deep down inside us all there is a creature who responds to danger signals such as bared fangs and whose instinct to run away remains almost irresistible. Fear is our natural safeguard, and the impulse to run has saved many lives.

THINGS THAT SHOULD NOT BE

Generation after generation add to the myths and stories of dragons, werewolves, vampires, and devils. Eventually, so many stories are told that they take on a life of their own. This creature is obviously a dragon, but it has been created by human hands. Many of the monsters that scare us are completely human inventions.

NIGHTMARES

When we sleep and our brain goes into neutral gear, random thoughts and things we try not to think about can sometimes bump together to produce nightmares. This picture, *The Nightmare* by Henry Fuseli, combines fears of the dark and the unknown.

CAVE PAINTINGS

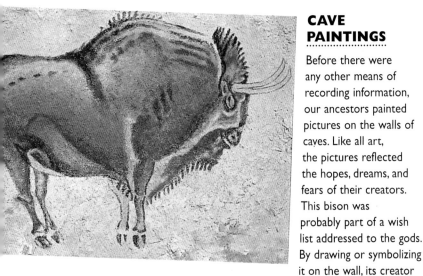

Before there were any other means of recording information, our ancestors painted pictures on the walls of caves. Like all art, the pictures reflected the hopes, dreams, and fears of their creators. This bison was probably part of a wish list addressed to the gods. By drawing or symbolizing it on the wall, its creator may have hoped to control his or her fear of a more powerful beast. This may explain our own enthusiasm for horror stories. Talking about, or giving a visible form to, what scares us can help make it less scary.

FOOD FOR THOUGHT

Monsters do not exist. However, we use them to represent our worst fears, and by confronting them we may help ourselves overcome them. While monsters are not real, our fears certainly are. There might be something at the window or sneaking up behind you. There is danger in the woods. There is violence in the world. It is wise to keep your fear instinct well tuned. Dragons do not exist, but dinosaurs did—and crocodiles still do! Sometimes, fact really is stranger and scarier than fiction.

GLOBAL HAUNTINGS

Although certain places seem to be a focus for supernatural activity, nowhere on Earth is off limits to ghosts. Wherever there are people, you can find accounts of ghosts. It seems that many ghosts repeatedly act out an action replay of a particular event in their previous lives, oblivious to all observers. Others are apparently benevolent and sometimes try to warn strangers of impending danger. However, occasionally ghosts can be malevolent.

SEEING DOUBLE

There are numerous stories of people who apparently have a double and are seen in two places at once. In 1845, in Livaria, Russia, one woman's double image actually appeared alongside her. A schoolteacher named Madame Sages was able to project an image of herself beyond her body. She used the technique in her classroom to maintain discipline, and while her ghostly image sat in front of the class, she would walk around or write on the blackboard. Her actions were witnessed not only by her students but also by her colleagues, who eventually asked for her dismissal.

THE SWEET SMELL OF VIOLETS

During the Zulu wars in South Africa in the 1900s, the prince imperial of France was killed. His body was returned to his family for burial and a mound of stones was erected as a memorial on the site where he had died. The following year, the prince's mother, Eugénie, wished to visit the battlefield where her son had died, but she could not find the memorial. While searching the undergrowth, she became aware of the scent of violets, which had been his favorite flower, and was therefore guided to the memorial.

CAR 42, WHERE ARE YOU?

The first Grand Prix to be held in Japan after World War II was in 1963 at the Suzuka circuit in Nagoya. The favorite was Masao Asano driving a car emblazoned with the number 42. During the race, Asano's car went out of control and he suffered a fatal crash. In Japanese, the number 42 translates as *shi ni*, which means "to die." Racing officials afterward banned the use of the number 42, but in the following year's Grand Prix event, marshals checking the cars as they passed noticed that a car bearing the number 42 was seen in eight out of the 25 laps.

CAUGHT IN TIME

In August 1901, two women visiting the Palace of Versailles walked toward the small private chateau of the queen of France, Marie Antoinette (1755–1793). Along the way, they sensed an oppressive atmosphere and passed strangely attired gardeners. A woman was sketching in the garden as they arrived. On a subsequent visit, the layout of the palace and gardens was different, and they were convinced that they must have slipped back in time on the previous occasion. They later identified the woman sketching as Marie Antoinette. Remarkably, the gardeners and the woman had stared at them as though they were actually there.

COFFINS THAT MOVED

In 1808, in Christ Church, Barbados, the family crypt of a Mrs. Goddard was bought by a plantation-owning family, the Chases. They buried two daughters in the stone tomb, but when it was reopened in 1812 to bury Mr. Chase, who, like one of his daughters, had committed suicide, the heavy lead coffins inside were found upended. The same happened at two more burials. In 1819, the governor of Barbados ordered the tomb to be sealed because it was creating fear among the local population. Following noises heard from within the tomb, it was reopened and the coffins were again in disarray, except Mrs. Goddard's. There was no sign of forced entry.

FOOD FOR THOUGHT

Human intervention could account for many supposed hauntings. In the case of the coffins that apparently moved by themselves, they could simply have been thrown into disarray by surviving relatives of the previous owner of the crypt, who might have resented the intrusion of strangers into the family grave. Tired minds can also create a dreamlike state so that we can easily become confused between the real world and that of daydreams, believing that we have seen things when, in fact, there is nothing there.

THIS HAUNTED ISLE

MULTIPLE HAUNTINGS

Many sites in Great Britain are haunted by more than one ghost. Destroyed by fire in 1939, Borley Rectory in Essex, England, was haunted by several ghosts, including a poltergeist, although doubt has now been cast upon their authenticity. Pluckley is said to be the most haunted village in Kent and perhaps in all of England. The most frequently seen ghost is the Red Lady, who haunts the local churchyard shown above, but there are at least a dozen other ghosts that have been reported.

For some reason, the British Isles appear to be the focus of a great deal of supernatural activity. Their populations have recorded more sightings of UFOs, ghosts, and other strange phenomena than any other region of comparable size in the world. Every year, there are almost more sightings of ghosts reported in Great Britain than in the rest of the world put together, making Great Britain the unofficial ghost capital of the world. Whatever the reasons for this high level of apparent spectral activity, it does mean that there is a wealth of material from all periods of history to investigate.

FEAR OF THE UNKNOWN

Ancient sites, such as the standing stones of Stonehenge in England, are often said to be haunted by spirits that protect their sanctity. One of the most common of these is the devil himself. It is said that anyone who desecrates the monument will meet an untimely end—perhaps being turned to stone!

THE WHITE LADY

Almost every castle in Great Britain is said to be haunted, many by unknown spirits. Rochester Castle in Kent is haunted by the ghost of Lady Blanche de Warenne. During a siege of the castle in 1264, she was accosted on the battlements by a rejected suitor, Gilbert de Clare. Ralph de Capo, to whom she was engaged, shot an arrow at her assailant. Deflected by de Clare's armor, it unfortunately killed Lady Blanche. Her ghost is now said to walk the battlements every year on the anniversary of her death.

LORE & ORDER

At Bramshill House in Hampshire, now used as a police training college, there have been so many ghostly encounters that even the worldly-wise police officers have accepted that the house must be haunted. In addition to the more usual ghosts, there are apparently rooms in the house that dogs will not enter, and even a path in the grounds that is haunted. One of the more pathetic of the many apparitions that haunt the house is a young girl who accidentally suffocated inside a trunk during a game of hide-and-seek one Christmas.

 FOOD FOR THOUGHT

Well known for their fertile imaginations, the British have produced some of the world's greatest works of literature and scientific invention. Perhaps their lively minds are all too willing to see mystery where none exists, embellish it, and pass it on as myth. The often murky weather conditions of the British Isles could account for some of the strange shadowy shapes that are sometimes thought to be ghosts.

FOOD FOR THOUGHT

Associating ghosts with the devil and haunting music were probably ploys used by early church authorities as they attempted to woo people away from pagan religions to follow the new true faith (as they saw it) of Christianity. Many European legends tell of ghosts haunting the ancient standing-stone monuments that were centers of pagan religions. Some say the stones themselves are the petrified remains of dancers who were turned to stone by the devil as they danced on the Sabbath.

THINGS THAT GO BUMP IN THE NIGHT

Ghosts are often accompanied by strange sounds. In fact, some ghosts seem only to be audible spirits who never manifest themselves in any visible form. Sounds associated with the earthly life of ghosts are common; so, too, is music. Sometimes, especially with poltergeists, a haunting is accompanied by obscene or blasphemous language. This is often voiced through living people, as if the ghosts were using them as a vehicle to express their anger. Audible ghosts are often accompanied by a sense of foreboding, as if they were predicting some tragic event. In Irish folklore, wailing banshees are female spirits said to warn of an impending death. Such spirits are common in many other cultures, including India and South America.

A PLANE MYSTERY

American musician Glen Miller is generally held to be the finest bandleader of his day. On December 15, 1944, he took an airplane from England to Paris, France, to arrange a series of concerts for the U.S. troops stationed there. The plane disappeared into thick fog and was never seen again. Several reports have described the outline of a small aircraft flying in the area where the plane is believed to have gone down. The sightings are accompanied by the ghostly sounds of a trombone.

THE DEVIL'S MUSIC

In more religious times, ghosts were often seen as the earthly manifestations of the devil himself. They were considered to be evil, especially if music accompanied a manifestation. There are many old stories of the devil attending festivities and disguising himself as a musician to tempt revelers to dance on the Sabbath (the seventh day of the week; a holy day). He played demonic music until the dancers either dropped from exhaustion or died.

PLAINTIVE SONG

Mermaids are creatures said to have no soul. In some stories, ghosts are transformed into mermaids and condemned to roam Earth in search of a soul. Legend tells of the sad, haunting songs these creatures use to lure people to them. There is a theory that these "ghosts of the sea" are no more than mirages formed by the air distortions caused by differing sea temperatures.

THE DRUMMER OF TIDWORTH

In Tidworth in Wiltshire, England, a famous ghost has been making regular appearances since the 1600s. The ghostly outline of a figure in the full military uniform of the day has often been seen on the old road to Devizes and heard playing a drum.

SCENTED SPIRITS

Some ghosts make their presence felt by scents and odors, as well as by sound. At Cotehele House in Cornwall, England, several ghosts have been reported over the years, including that of a white lady. Ghostly music is sometimes heard, and visitors often ask about the strong herbal fragrance that seems to permeate the entire house. The scent seems to come and go at random, at all times of the day.

ASTRAL PROJECTION

Most religions believe in a spirit world (or astral plane) to which the souls of the dead return. It is not a separate place in the heavens but is thought to exist all around us at a level of consciousness of which we are normally unaware. The astral body, or spirit of a person, is said to leave the body during sleep and at death in order to enter this other level of existence. Ghosts may be astral projections of dead people who have become trapped between this world and the next. Until released in some way, they are unable to pass fully into the spirit world.

 **FOOD FOR THOUGHT**

It is possible that victims of violent crimes, such as murder, generate an excess of chemicals such as adrenaline or a high charge of electrical activity within their bodies. In some way this may impart an image or energy field into the surrounding air. Under the right conditions, this image might be seen as a hologram, but it is merely an image with no physical substance.

ISLE OF THE BLESSED

In Celtic mythology, when King Arthur was about to die, he was transported in a boat to Avalon, the Isle of the Blessed. According to the legend, Arthur did not die but recovered and returned to fight the enemies of his country whenever he was needed. Unable to rest lest he be called upon, the ghost of Arthur has sometimes been seen in Cam valley in Somerset, England, the supposed site of the king's last earthly battle.

RESTLESS SOULS

The most common reason given for a ghost manifesting itself is that the spirit or soul of the dead person is troubled and unable to rest. This state of transience is believed to have many causes, but all are in some way connected to a sense of injustice, or perhaps guilt that in life the person did not do all that he or she could have to protect someone. Injustice might be felt by the victim of a violent murder who returns again and again to the scene of the crime, apparently unable to rest until the murderer has been revealed. Alternatively, a ghost might simply be someone who was not ready to die and felt aggrieved that their time on Earth had been cut short.

PHANTOM CARGO

In Papua New Guinea, natives are often seen scanning the horizon for "phantom cargo." They wait for dead relatives to come in great canoes (nowadays, ships and airplanes, too) full of goods that will enrich their lives. In the past, missionaries who brought items from the civilized world were sometimes allowed to settle in Papua because the natives mistook them for the ghosts of their dead ancestors.

HEADLESS HAUNTINGS

Headless ghosts are common, presumably because the people felt a strong sense of injustice about meeting such a violent end. In the past, the Tower of London was the scene of many executions and is reputed to be the single most haunted building in the world. Similarly, in Paris at the time of the French Revolution (1789–1799), the site of the executions is reputedly haunted by several headless ghosts, including Louis XVI and Marie Antoinette.

MYTHICAL GODS

In Nordic mythology, one of the most feared apparitions was Odin, the god of war. Leading a pack of dogs on the "Wild Hunt," Odin rode across the night sky in search of lost souls. The apparition usually foretold of an impending death.

CITY OF GOD

While camped outside Rome in A.D. 312, Emperor Constantine saw a vision of a fiery cross in the midday sky. An inscription on it urged him to attack the city. He carried out the attack and was victorious. In gratitude to the Holy Spirit, which he claimed to have seen, he ordered that Christianity become the official religion of the Roman Empire.

CUSTER'S LAST STAND

In June 1876, American Civil War hero General George Custer was killed fighting the Sioux Indians at the Battle of Little Bighorn. One month earlier, as Custer had ridden out of Fort Abraham Lincoln at the start of the expedition, people in the fort saw half the regiment apparently rise up into the sky and then vanish. It may have been a mirage caused by the heat of the sun, but around half the 7th Cavalry were subsequently massacred in the battle.

SPECTRAL ARMIES

In the past, when belief in myths and legends was greater than it is today, ghosts tended to be of a more spectacular nature. Visions of gods or heroic figures would appear, and spectral armies fighting battles in the sky were once quite a common occurrence. Today, such visions are rare; in modern hauntings, people tend to see only one ghost. This would seem to indicate a link between the type of apparition seen and the background and experience of the person who witnessed it. There are stories of King Arthur and the ancient Nordic gods Odin and Thor fighting great ghostly battles. These spectral events could have been mirages of actual battles, while others were perhaps warnings of battles yet to be fought.

DRAKE'S DRUM

Sir Francis Drake (1540–1596) used a drum to muster the crew of the *Golden Hind* for battle. According to legend, on his deathbed Drake promised to return and fight for England if ever the drum were beaten at the approach of an enemy. During World War II, stories circulated of warships being miraculously saved from disaster after the ghostly sounds of drumming were heard. However, Drake's drum has never been carried aboard any ship since its return to England in the 1500s.

BOWMEN OF MONS

During World War I (1914–1918), the first battle fought by British forces was in Mons, Belgium, where they were grossly outnumbered by the German army. A report in the newspapers told of a miraculous vision that appeared in the sky above the battlefield, urging on the British troops. The report claimed the vision was St. George and his bowmen, but eyewitnesses from both sides told of an army carrying swords, projected onto the sky like a movie. No sounds were heard, but the vision was witnessed by many individuals on the battlefield and has been interpreted by some as divine intervention.

ACTION REPLAY

In August 1942, during World War II, Allied troops launched an attack on the German-held town of Dieppe on the coast of Normandy in France. It was a prelude to the D-day landings, and the mission was a success. Nine years later, two women on vacation near Dieppe were woken early one morning by the sound of gunfire. For the next three hours, they listened in stunned silence as the battle of nine years before was reenacted. Their accounts were afterward compared to official records of the battle and found to be very similar.

 **FOOD FOR THOUGHT**

The intensity of a life-or-death battle inevitably causes the release of large amounts of adrenaline in the participants. Stories such as the bowmen of Mons may have been the result of mass hysteria or borne out of a collective memory of some long-past scene. People often see what they want to see. Three different observers of the same event, say a soldier, a priest, and a scientist, will each explain it in terms in which they relate. The soldier may see an army of ghost soldiers in the sky; the priest the divine light of God; while the scientist may see ball lightning or interpret the others' visions as products of overwrought minds.

UNKNOWN FORCES

Most ghosts appear to be benign and cause no physical harm. However, some spirits are far from passive and can inflict actual bodily injuries or, in extreme cases, death. The most common form of such malevolent behavior is poltergeist activity. There are also many reports of people falling victim to invisible assailants. One extreme case in 1761 in Ventimiglia, Italy, involved a woman who was attacked by an unseen force. Her body was literally torn apart in the presence of her four companions, who remained unharmed.

HAIR TODAY, GONE TOMORROW

Between 1876–1879, the province of Nanjing, China, suffered a strange yet oddly recurring phenomenon in Chinese history. An invisible assailant ran amuk cutting off people's pigtails. Sometimes a shadowy figure was briefly seen, while at other times the hair was invisibly grabbed from behind and sheared off. Similar happenings were reported in Canada in 1899 and in London, England, in 1922.

POLTERGEISTS

Poltergeist activity often includes objects being hurled through the air, but sometimes they also appear from out of nowhere. In 1998, all the items shown here "fell" into a house in the Northern Territory of Australia within a period of two or three hours. The knife flew past an investigator who was in the house at the time, narrowly missing his ear.

FOOD FOR THOUGHT

There is plenty of evidence of malevolent poltergeist activity, but the source of this "power" remains a mystery. Most poltergeist activity is centered around young teenage girls at the time when their bodies are undergoing immense physical changes. The girls may themselves be the source of the poltergeist activity as a result of heightened mental and chemical activity affecting the environment around them.

CAUGHT ON CAMERA

This still from 1967 video footage taken in Rosenheim, Germany, shows a light fixture in a lawyer's office swinging unaided. No physical cause could be attributed to the phenomenon. The telephone system also behaved strangely. All four of the office telephones would suddenly ring without reason, and strange power surges were recorded. Sigmund Adam, the lawyer, called in experts to help. The source of these mysterious happenings seemed to be his secretary, a 19-year-old woman. When she left, the activity stopped.

HOUSE CLEARANCE

The furniture in this house in Dodleston, England, was repeatedly piled into one corner of the room by an unknown force while the owners were out of the room. On one occasion in 1983, computer messages were also received, purportedly transmitted by a man living in the 1500s. Perhaps this is a case of parallel worlds where people from other time spans or dimensions appear to be sharing the same space as ourselves.

BODILY HARM

In 1926, this 13-year-old Romanian girl, Eleonore Zugun, suffered horrific injuries at the hands of an invisible force. Witnesses described seeing her throat being squeezed as though she were being strangled. On other occasions, bite and scratch marks appeared spontaneously on her face and neck.

The most obvious explanation for ghosts seen at sea is that sailors, subjected to long voyages, often in rough waters, can become disoriented or unbalanced. This could distort the sensory perception of seamen and lead them to believe they are actually seeing things that are not there, in much the same way as a hallucination.

THE *FLYING DUTCHMAN*

In 1680, the *Flying Dutchman* set sail from Amsterdam, Netherlands, to Batavia in the Dutch East Indies. The ship was severely damaged in a violent storm off the Cape of Good Hope, but the captain refused to turn back. His arrogance and blasphemous behavior was said to have caused God to condemn him to sail the seas forever. Now considered an ill omen, the phantom ship has since been seen many times, including by the future king of England, George V, in 1881.

PHANTOM SHIPS

Over the centuries, the world's oceans have been the scene of many shipping disasters, and the loss of life has often given rise to tales of ghosts and phantom ships. One area especially associated with mystery is the Bermuda Triangle in the North Atlantic Ocean. Hundreds of ships (and airplanes) have simply disappeared there without a trace, and several ghost ships have been reported in the area. When sightings of phantom ships are reported by credible witnesses such as King George V, who as a young naval officer sighted the *Flying Dutchman*, we are forced to take the stories seriously rather than dismiss them as delusions of sailors who have drunk too much rum.

ALL AT SEA

This rare photograph is believed to show the images of two dead seamen as witnessed by the ship's entire crew. In the 1920s, the oil tanker SS *Watertown* was sailing from the Pacific coast of the U.S. to the Panama Canal. Two of the crew members died in an accident and were buried at sea. The next day and for several days afterward, two phantom faces that resembled the dead crew were seen in the waves behind the ship. They always appeared in the same position for a few moments and then disappeared. The likenesses materialized during the next two voyages of the ship but were never seen again.

AIRSHIPS

From all corners of the globe there have been reports of mysterious airships—not the great gas-filled zeppelins of the early 1900s but wooden galleons in full sail drifting across the sky. One such apparition was witnessed in Papua New Guinea in 1959 by the entire staff of a religious mission.

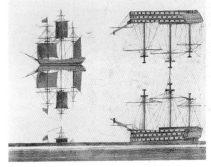

SEA RESCUE

In 1895, Joshua Slocum, the first man to sail around the world single-handedly, claimed to have been rescued by a 16th-century ghost. Taken ill during a ferocious storm in the Azores, the American seaman collapsed in his bunk. When he awoke, Slocum saw at the helm of his ship, the *Spray*, a seaman who said he was the pilot of the *Pinta*, a caravel (like this replica) that had sailed with Christopher Columbus in 1492. The apparition could be dismissed as delirium, except that the *Spray* had remained precisely on course for some 90 mi. (144km).

A VENGEFUL GHOST?

In 1908, the British warship HMS *Gladiator* (left) sank in Portsmouth harbor after colliding with the American steam liner *St. Paul*, with the loss of 27 lives. Incredibly, exactly ten years later to the hour, the *St. Paul* inexplicably capsized in the Hudson River in New York City and sank with the loss of four lives. Claims of sabotage were rife, but because of the amazing coincidence of date and time, many believed that the ghost of a dead seaman from the *Gladiator* was responsible.

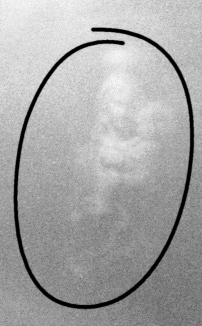

HEAVENLY VISIONS

From time to time, someone reports seeing a
miraculous vision. These visions come in a
variety of forms, including dreams, ghostly
appearances, and miraculous images.
In 1980, Ivy Wilson photographed this
rainbow in Woombye in southeastern
Queensland, Australia. When she had
the film developed, she noticed this
image of the Virgin Mary and child.
The photograph was not taken
through glass, so it could not
have been a reflection.

SPIRIT IN
THE SKY

It is not uncommon
for religious visions
or holy spirits to
appear in the clouds.
This vision of Jesus
Christ is said to have
been photographed
during a bombing
mission in the Korean
War (1950–1953).
Ghosts are often
described as if they
are made of the same
matter as clouds, and
like clouds they can
appear for a few
moments before
vaporizing into thin
air. The soul has also
been likened to a
cloud that vaporizes
as it leaves the body.

HOLY GHOSTS

The church is usually associated with banishing unwelcome spirits, but it also has its fair share of its own ghosts. Many of these apparitions take the form of miraculous images, or visions of Jesus Christ, the Virgin Mary, or the saints. Besides these religious visions, the church tends to explain ghosts as restless spirits whose souls, for one reason or another, are unable to pass over into the afterlife, and they blame the unruly behavior of poltergeists on the devil. Most religions classify good and evil spirits in much the same way. The Christian Church calls the spirit of God the Holy Ghost.

METHODIST IN THEIR MADNESS

Toward the end of the 1600s, the Wesley family, the founders of the Methodist Church, moved into the Old Rectory in Epworth in Yorkshire, England. The rectory became the center of much activity and religious fervor. This may have unsettled a Catholic spirit, because, for a short period during 1715–1716, the house suffered what may have been poltergeist activity. Incidents were many and varied, including a corn grinder and mechanical spit that started unaided, the sounds of a rocking cradle, mysterious knocking noises, and doors that flew open suddenly. Headless animals were seen, and members of the family were hurled against walls. The activity subsided gradually, but incidents still occasionally occur there.

DREAMTIME

Aboriginal Australians treat their dead relatives with extreme reverence. They have no fear of death, and the ghosts of their dead are welcome to join in their rituals and celebrations. Aboriginals periodically perform magic rituals to renew their relationship with their dead ancestors, who are encouraged to revisit their earthly tribal lands.

GETTING THE HABIT

Everywhere in the world, there are ruined churches and abbeys allegedly haunted by monks and nuns. A Siberian peasant monk, Grigori Rasputin is said to haunt the old royal palace in Moscow, Russia. Having gained the confidence of Czar Nicholas II and Empress Alexandra, Rasputin virtually ruled Russia prior to the revolution. He made many enemies and was murdered by a group of noblemen in 1916. His ghost still walks the corridors of power, supposedly seeking revenge.

FOOD FOR THOUGHT

Seeing visions in cloud shapes has a rational explanation. Known as eidetic images, such visions can be exceptionally vivid but are thought to be recalled from something previously seen. If we stare long and hard at some unrelated surface, many of us will begin to see things—such as faces among the patterns on wallpaper, in the flickering flames of a fire, or in the sky. The human mind works hard to "read" what is being seen and may eventually interpret abstract shapes as a familiar object or perhaps a desired supernatural being.

LITERARY SPOOKING

GHOST STORIES

Sometimes ghosts were used as a literary device to put across an idea or message, especially in politically sensitive times when the depiction of contemporary events might have been prohibited by a repressive regime. This Japanese woodcut is a piece of veiled war propaganda expressed by having a ghost appear to the samurai warrior Kingo Chunagon Hideaki during the 19th-century civil wars in Japan.

People who have never seen a ghost might find it difficult to believe in them, but many of us keep an open mind about their existence. However, we enjoy the inclusion of fictional ghosts in books and plays. A ghostly haunting can be a useful device used by authors to force a character to atone for some misdemeanor. In such plots, the haunted characters usually become so eaten up by their sense of guilt that they cause their own downfalls. These literary ghosts can take on a real and familiar presence in our imagination—almost to the point of our believing in them. This may help keep alive the possibility of ghosts truly existing.

GHOULISH GHOSTS

Ghosts are big business. Many movies featuring them have attracted huge audiences. Some, like *Casper* (right) and *Ghostbusters,* are lighthearted spoofs, but others, such as *The Exorcist*, are said to be based on real events. *The Exorcist* tells the story of a young girl possessed by the devil. When the movie was shown in a theater in Australia, several of the audience members left before the movie had even started because of strange occurrences in the theater.

GHOSTLY INTERVENTION

Dante's celebrated poem *The Divine Comedy* may never have been published were it not for the intervention of his own ghost. When he died in 1321, everyone supposed his epic poem was unfinished because, despite an exhaustive search, the missing part of the manuscript could not be found. One night, however, Dante's ghost appeared to his son, Jacopo, in a dream, revealing the secret hiding place. It has been suggested that Jacopo may have finished the poem himself and used the ploy of the ghost to pass off the work as his father's.

GUILTY CONSCIENCE

Many authors have used a ghost in their plots to make their characters face up to the consequences of past actions. In *A Christmas Carol* by Charles Dickens, Ebenezer Scrooge is visited by the ghosts of Christmases past, present, and future to make him atone for being a selfish old miser. William Shakespeare used a ghost scene to make Macbeth repent his murder of Banquo. Dickens himself was buried in Westminster Abbey in London, England, yet his ghost is said to haunt a graveyard in Rochester, where the author had wanted to be buried.

GHOSTLY VISIT

Swiss psychiatrist Carl Jung (1875–1961) had a great interest in the afterlife and wrote effusively about it in his autobiography. He claimed, among other things, that the ghost of a recently departed friend had visited him in a dream and taken him on a tour of the friend's study. The following day, Jung visited the man's widow and asked to see the study, which he had never visited. To his amazement, it was exactly as he had envisaged in his dream.

GHOSTLY BEASTS

Animals feature prominently in accounts of ghost sightings. Sometimes, ghosts of dead pets appear in much the same way as conventional ghosts. Some ghost animals are seen as signals of ill fortune. Perhaps of more interest is the apparent ability of animals to sense the presence of ghosts before humans are aware of them. This may indicate that animals have a type of ESP (extrasensory perception). Dogs often will not enter a haunted room or, if they do, their hairs will rise as if they detect an intruder. Because animals often possess senses far beyond the normal human range, they may detect the changes to electromagnetic fields that are often associated with reports of ghosts.

WHITE BIRDS

Although associated with love, peace, and life itself, white doves are sometimes the signals of impending death. Ghostly white birds have been seen fluttering above the beds of those close to death. Sometimes they are seen by the dying person, at other times by independent witnesses, but they always foretell a death in the household. Similar sightings have been reported from widely different places such as Ireland and Japan.

FOOD FOR THOUGHT

When confronted by something unexpected, most people react with fear. Large black cats have been seen in locations around the world where such wild animals should not exist. It is all too easy to assume that these beasts are in some way supernatural. However, a growing body of evidence suggests that large feral cats, such as black panthers, may have escaped from zoos or private collections and somehow managed to survive in urban areas.

THE DEVIL

Most cultures of the world have their equivalent of the devil (as he is known in Christianity). He usually represents the opposite of all that is good. Seeing him brings bad luck or death. He often takes the form of a creature who is half man, half beast. Many people believe that all animal ghosts are really the devil in disguise.

PHANTOM CANINES

The most commonly seen animal phantoms are black dogs that are usually, but not always, associated with evil. They are often believed to be affiliated with the devil, and those who encounter them are frequently injured. Black-dog manifestations are also said to predict an impending death. However, it used to be the custom in medieval Europe to bury a dog in new graveyards to protect the souls of the dead.

SACRED RATS

The temple of Karai Ma in Bikaner in the Indian state of Rajasthan is infested with rats. Karai Ma is the goddess of a caste of professional poets called Charans. Whenever a Charan dies, he is believed to return to the temple as a rat, and when a rat dies, it is said to return as a poet.

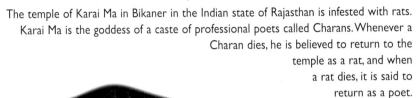

GHOSTLY FELINE

Not all ghostly sightings of animals are of a sinister nature. At a house called King John's Hunting Lodge in Somerset, England, the ghost of a friendly tabby cat (probably the much-loved pet of a previous owner) has often been seen. It appears to enter a second-floor paneled room through a closed door and curls up happily on the floor before disappearing.

SCREECHING OWLS

Owls have traditionally been associated with death. Ghosts of owls that appear at the window of a house and then mysteriously disappear are thought to foretell a death in the family.

A HOUSE BUILT BY GHOSTS

Winchester House in California was built to appease the spirit world. William Winchester, the founder of the famous rifle company, died in 1881. His widow, who had recently also lost their only child, became troubled by spirits. A spiritualist told her that the souls of all those killed by a Winchester rifle had banded together to seek revenge. The spirits insisted that she build a house to their specifications, without stopping until she died. In 1884, Mrs. Winchester bought a small farmhouse. Day and night for the rest of her life, she expanded it according to the bizarre instructions of the spirits. It has many strange features such as staircases that rise to the ceiling and doors that lead nowhere.

DAY OF THE DEAD

In Mexico, the Purépecha Indians perform elaborate ceremonies not only to venerate the memories of dead ancestors but also to actively encourage their spirits to appear. In November each year, the dead have divine permission to visit their living relatives during the Day of the Dead celebrations.

FOOD FOR THOUGHT

Exorcisms are commonly performed by priests of all religions to rid people and places of evil spirits. This could be a simple matter of autosuggestion (mind over matter). Superstitious people can be possessed by a spirit only because they are willing to believe such a thing is possible. Just as people can convince themselves that they are possessed, they can go to see a priest in whom they have absolute faith and likewise convince themselves that the priest is able to exorcise the evil spirit. In reality, they were probably never possessed at all; it was all in their own minds.

GLOBAL ATTITUDES

Cultures around the world have different attitudes to ghosts. Westerners tend to fear ghosts as the restless spirits of the dead, whereas in many supposedly less-sophisticated cultures, the ghosts of ancestors are celebrated and welcomed. However, if the spirits of the dead are in some way violated, they might exact some form of revenge. In 1942, a man named Adrian Brooks was posted as district officer to Kasama in what is now Zambia. He inadvertently violated the sacred burial ground of the chiefs of a local tribe, the Bemba, by taking photographs of the site. Witch doctors warned him that he had angered the spirits of their leaders and that their ghosts would return to kill him. He scoffed at the warning, but three days later, he suffered a bizarre fatal accident when a flagpole fell on him.

SPIRIT POSSESSION

In voodoo ceremonies, participants actively encourage the ghosts or spirits of the dead to possess them. Rhythmic drumming sends dancers into such a frenzy that they go into a trancelike state. The combination of powerful autosuggestion from a witch doctor and hallucinogenic drugs work together to produce a powerful effect.

DEMONIC POSSESSION

Exorcisms are performed in all religions to banish unwelcome spirits. This Dayak shaman from Borneo, Indonesia, is performing an exorcism on an unfortunate individual who has been possessed by a demon.

HALLOWEEN

In ancient times, October 31 marked the end of the old year, when the veil between this world and the afterlife was at its thinnest. On this night, the spirits of the dead were able to leave their graves and wander Earth. The Christian Church adopted the festival as All Hallows Eve, and despite its pagan origins, the night is still celebrated, especially in the United States, where it involves the lighthearted ritual of trick-or-treating.

GHOST BUSTING

However skeptical we may be about ghosts, the vast number of reported sightings has encouraged some people to take the subject seriously. Scientists have turned their attention to investigating paranormal phenomena, using a growing array of equipment and recording methods. Current research suggests that some form of energy (a byproduct of electricity or magnetism) may produce ghostly manifestations. Until more conclusive evidence can be found, however, many will continue to believe in ghosts as supernatural beings from another dimension.

CHILL FACTOR

One of the most commonly experienced phenomena during poltergeist activity is a dramatic fluctuation in temperature, as was recorded during an investigation in Mulhouse, France. When ghosts appear, not only is the electromagnetic field altered but the ambient temperature can drop by 35 degrees. No wonder people who see ghosts often report a feeling of cold shivers. Such a drop in temperature can be recorded on portable infrared thermometers.

CAUSE & EFFECT

Ghostly manifestations often occur together with recordable fluctuations in Earth's electromagnetic fields. Researchers use special equipment (above) to detect such changes, and some believe that these indicate the presence of ghosts. Others, including scientists at the Laurentian University of Sudbury in Ontario, Canada, believe that natural fluctuations in Earth's electromagnetic fields can cause the human brain to hallucinate and thus "create" its own ghosts. If this is true, sites that are subject to magnetic fluctuations are likely to seem especially haunted.

FOOD FOR THOUGHT

Despite the increasing sophistication of modern technology, including photographic and recording equipment, there is no conclusive proof of the existence of ghosts. If they exist, some form of evidence would surely have come to light by now. After all, a vast number of ghosts are claimed to wander Earth. It seems unlikely that ghosts are the spirits of dead people. Most reported ghosts are probably no more than self-induced images grown out of long-held superstitions.

CAUGHT ON FILM

Some researchers use infrared cameras to detect radiation from spirits and also to photograph in the dark. More commonly, ghostly figures are unexpectedly caught in a photograph. The example shown here was taken in 1995 during the photographing of a fire at Wem Town Hall in Shropshire, England. When the picture was developed, this ghostly image appeared. It is thought that it can be linked to a previous fire in Wem in 1677, caused accidentally by a young girl. Critics suggest that such photos are merely accidental double exposures, reflections, or even blatant frauds.

ARE YOU SITTING COMFORTABLY?

This famous picture of a séance in 1872 shows John Beattie in a trance state, supposedly conjuring up a spirit. However convincing such images may be, not one indisputable photograph of a ghost or spirit has ever been produced. Many mediums have been exposed as frauds, and skeptics believe that séance participants are easily deceived because they see and hear what they choose to.

CLASSICAL MONSTERS

CLASH OF THE TITANS

The movie *Clash of the Titans* presents a very different version of the legendary kraken (sea monster). In the movie, it is portrayed as a monstrous amphibian, a lot like the city-stomping Godzilla. Here, it is coming to steal away the sacrificial victim Andromeda. In the original legend, a giant whale is sent for Andromeda.

Classical mythology provides us with many scary monsters. Some, which represented supposedly magical forces, were borne out of an ancient awe of natural phenomena such as tidal waves and earthquakes. Others gave a monstrous form to human characteristics—such as the vicious power of gossip personified in the mythical Rumor, a winged creature with 1,000 eyes and 1,000 ears. Since they are derived from Latin, even the words we use for being scared are rooted in the classical world. A *monstrum* is a warning, a signal, an example of something shocking designed to keep us from straying from the path. Monsters can also be used to scare children into doing as they are told. *Horrere* (to bristle)—that terrible feeling when your hair stands on end—is the Latin word that gave us *horror*.

SIRENS

Half woman, half bird, these mythical monsters lured seafarers onto deadly rocks with their beautiful singing. But they were thwarted by Odysseus, who filled his crew's ears with wax and tied himself to the mast of his ship so he that would not be tempted. The Sirens were eventually destroyed by Orpheus, who sung a sweeter song. Defeated, they flung themselves into the water, where they were turned into rocks.

THE MINOTAUR

A man with the head of a bull—supposedly the result of a curse on Minos, the king of Crete—the Minotaur lived in the center of a great maze. Each year, the Athenians had to send seven boys and seven girls to be sacrificed to the Minotaur, or risk invasion. The Minotaur was eventually slain by Theseus, a Greek hero who went in disguise as one of the sacrificial victims. Theseus fell in love with Ariadne, the daughter of the king of Crete, who gave him a sword and a ball of thread by which he could retrace his steps through the maze.

HYDRA

The hero Hercules was told to defeat the Hydra, a snakelike monster with nine heads. Each time he struck off one of the heads with his club, two more would grow in its place. But Hercules managed to burn away eight of the heads before burying the ninth (which was immortal) under a rock.

MEDUSA

The Gorgons were three terrifying creatures who had snakes instead of hair, as well as wings, claws, and enormous teeth. Two of them, Stheno and Euryale, were immortal, but the most famous was the mortal Medusa. Once a beautiful girl, she was turned into a monster by the jealous Greek goddess Athena. Medusa became so ugly that one look at her face would turn the viewer to stone. The hero Perseus defeated her by looking only at her reflection. He was then able to cut off her head. But even after death, the sight of her ugliness continued to turn anyone who looked at her to stone.

FOOD FOR THOUGHT

Superstition and religion were the science of the ancient world. But these stories, the entertainments of the time, were often rooted in real events. The people of Crete worshiped a bull god. Perhaps this, coupled with a fear of invasion, was twisted over time to become the tale of the Minotaur. The story of the Sirens contains its own explanation. The Sirens were dangerous rocks, and the story warned sailors of their presence. And what's worse than a snake? A snake with nine heads, of course! How ugly is the ugliest person you can think of? So ugly you'd die if you looked at them!

VAMPIRES

ELIZABETH BÁTHORY

Bram Stoker's Count Dracula may have been a composite character inspired by Vlad the Impaler and Countess Elizabeth Báthory. Arrested in 1610 for murdering young girls, she believed bathing in the blood of her victims would keep her looking youthful.

FOOD FOR THOUGHT

The idea of vampires is really quite silly, but they do combine several important elements. There's the historical aspect, plus the fear of a powerful individual who abuses those less fortunate than himself. But, ultimately, vampire stories are rooted in a fear of the dead and in the observation of what happens after people die. Their skin shrinks back slightly, making teeth and nails look longer; they become pale, as if their blood has been drained away. A wolf or a bat is just an animal, but say it's possessed by a dead soul and you have a scary story. And a cloud of gas? Might this be methane gas rising over a graveyard from a decaying body beneath the earth? There's a rational explanation for everything except perhaps why people find these stories so compelling.

Supposedly the ghost of a heretic (a person who holds different beliefs to those of the established church) or a criminal, a vampire comes out of its grave at night in the guise of a bat to suck blood from people as they sleep. As a result, the victims become vampires themselves. The most famous vampire is from the novel *Dracula* (1897) by Bram Stoker. Count Dracula was based on two historical figures, but legends of vampirism existed long before the book was written. Some myths say vampires cannot be reflected in a mirror because they have no souls. Also, old mirrors were made with silver, and because Jesus Christ was betrayed for 30 pieces of silver, silver was thought to reflect evil.

VERONICA CARLSON · BARBARA EWING · BARRY ANDREWS · EWAN HOOPER

MODERN VAMPIRES

Modern myths say vampires can change into wolves, bats, or even clouds of gas. They have long fangs for sinking into human flesh and drinking blood, and they have to stay out of sunlight. They can be killed only by a stake through the heart.

VLAD THE IMPALER

Vlad V of Wallachia (1431–1476) was born in Transylvania. He was a brutal warlord reputed to have killed more than 100,000 people. Stories tell of him nailing hats to people's heads, skinning them alive, and, most famously, impaling them on upright stakes—for which he earned the nickname Vlad the Impaler. He was also called Vlad, son of the dragon (or Dracula). His behavior made some people think he had sold his soul to the devil and led to rumors that he would never be admitted into heaven. Murdered in 1476, his tomb was reported empty, and the legends began.

THE VAMPIRE BAT

This humble bat scrapes a hole in an animal's skin and drinks its blood. In that sense, it is not much different from a mosquito (just bigger), but the blood drinking was associated with vampirism and the name stuck.

KALI

Kali, the Hindu goddess of death, is one of the most fearsome creatures of mythology. Even today, animals are sacrificed to her, but in the past it was human beings who were offered to appease her anger. She is usually depicted as a black-skinned, red-eyed demon with four arms, wearing a necklace of skulls. The Indian city of Kolkata (Calcutta) is said to derive from *kalighat*, the "staircase of Kali," which her worshipers use to enter the Ganges River.

GARGOYLES

Originally simple spouts for draining water from the roofs of churches, gargoyles (the French word for *gullet* is *gargouille*) were carved into a variety of grotesque stone demons. In the 600s, a great dragon named Gargouille was believed to live in the Seine River in Paris.

DEMONS & DEVILS

The Hindu *deva* and the Greek *daimon* are both creatures of myth that have been changed over time into our words *devil* and *demon*. Once simple paranormal beings with both good and bad natures, they were proclaimed as wholly evil with the ascendence of Christianity. The Christian term *Satan* comes from the Hebrew word *shatana*, which means "adversary." In the Bible, Satan is identified in Revelations as meaning the same thing as the dragon and the serpent. In other words: the devil. Satan is the supreme evil spirit: the enemy and tempter of man and the ruler of hell.

PAN

Half man, half goat, the ancient Greek god Pan became a model for many Christian images of the devil. The cloven hooves and horns seem to have been carried over into the modern idea of the devil. We get the word *panic* from the terrible fear his appearance was intended to strike into nonbelievers.

FALLEN ANGELS

Biblical angels may do the bidding of God, but in the Old Testament, this often meant laying waste to armies, killing children, and striking down people with diseases. John Milton linked this with the idea of Lucifer and wrote

the book *Paradise Lost*, a tale of Lucifer's expulsion from heaven. The ousted angel and his followers prefer to be rulers in hell than servants in heaven.

LUCIFER

"How art thou fallen from Heaven, O Lucifer, star of the morning," said the Bible's Book of Isaiah, poetically linking the death of the king of Babylon with the arrival of the morning star, Venus (*Lucifer*: light bringer). Over time, this phrase was confused with Satan himself, and the name *Lucifer* came to be identified with evil.

 FOOD FOR THOUGHT

What great stories! If people at war pretend their enemies are inhuman (to avoid admitting that they are committing murder), the tales of ancient wars can fast become tales of demonic attacks. Like the Sirens of ancient Greece, demons and devils are simply symbols of evil and temptation, perhaps even of past enemies. Blaming a devil for a wicked deed seems easier than taking responsibility for it.

39

FROM JINNI TO GENIE

Middle Eastern jinni were thought to have been created from fire 2,000 years before Adam was made out of clay. They entered Western mythology as genies, although their original destructive powers have been tempered over time to offer little more than the granting of wishes.

 **FOOD FOR THOUGHT**

Some real people are born small—the average height of the Congo Mbuti tribe is a mere 4 ft. 5 in. (137cm)—but they have no relation to the mythical beings shown here. It is said that elves and fairies are wounded by iron. This may refer to the local peoples of Bronze Age culture being pushed into the forests and wilderness by invading Iron Age tribes. Other fairy tales seem to be remnants of pagan religions, belittled by the arrival of Christianity and mutated as they were passed by word of mouth through the generations.

Ultimately, the simplest explanation works best—if you can't think of a good reason for some act of mischief, blame an evil spirit. Of course, mischief-makers have to be small; if they were giants, everyone else would have seen them, too. The sound of mice scurrying behind the walls may have added credence to the ancient legends.

GOBLINS, KOBOLDS, & SPIRITS

Perhaps with their origins in the desire of children to have something smaller than themselves in the world, the "little people" are another type of monster. Sometimes demonic, they are more often impudent or mischievous rogues who dwell in our houses, holes in trees, and other nooks and crannies. The mythologies of most cultures include stories of little people such as gnomes, goblins, kobolds, and leprechauns. They are often portrayed as misshapen old men who hoarded treasures. The most famous are perhaps the Scandinavian Norse dwarves. They had their own king and were not unfriendly to humans but could be very vindictive and mischievous. The Norse word *alfar* may have given us the English word *elf*.

DWARVES

According to Norse mythology, dwarves began their existence as maggots living in the flesh of a giant. Found in the mythology of most races, they were said to live beneath the earth or in rocks and to be the guardians of its precious metals and stones. Dwarves were sometimes believed to help human beings. Carved on this stone tomb, four dwarves are depicted supporting the sky over a dead Viking.

KOBOLDS

Another type of dwarf said to live in German mines were kobolds, who did everything they could to make life difficult for silver miners. They would cause cave-ins, explosions, and rockfalls. Miners lived in dread of their activities. Sometimes, they mixed silver ore with their own magic metal, and this became known as cobalt.

FAIRIES

We think of fairies as the tiny butterfly-like creatures we know from Victorian children's stories. But in earlier times they were something to be afraid of—roaming creatures said to steal babies from their mothers' arms. Fairies began as inhabitants of the dark forests, creatures who would lure unsuspecting travelers to their doom. In the Middle Ages, they were symbols of temptation; they lured people to commit sins without revealing that there would be a horrible price to pay.

ELVES

Although sometimes allies of humans, elves were notoriously unreliable, always likely to go back on bargains and twist the words of promises. In the Middle Ages, when a child was born dead or disabled, it was believed that fairies or elves had swapped the human child for one of their own—a changeling. It is often said that elves are hurt by iron, a metal said in China to "wound the eyes of dragons."

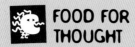

FOOD FOR THOUGHT

There is an element of truth in these stories. Some people do grow to be very tall, but that doesn't make them monsters. Tall people often suffer from a variety of ailments, including bad backs, stoops, and tunnel vision. The latter may explain why Goliath did not notice a rock flying at him from the side. But what about the really big giants of legend? Many are folktales that grew out of the need to explain strange natural phenomena. Most, as usual, are products of the human mind. In the earliest days of childhood, we are loomed over by adults so much taller than we are that, to a tiny child, they could seem like giants.

REAL-LIFE GIANTS

In this photo, these two towering men are standing beside tiny Professor James Ricalton in Kashmir, India, but how *giant* are they? Perhaps the professor is actually quite short—the "giants" are much taller than average but not excessively so. People of great height are not unheard of, but the picture is oddly posed. Professor Ricalton has taken off his hat; while the two "giants" wear turbans that make them look taller. The image is impressive, but parts of it are cosmetic—a lot like a puffer fish that pretends to be bigger than it is. Great size, or the illusion of it, is used in the natural world to scare away potential predators.

GOLIATH

A huge champion of the Philistines in the Bible, Goliath was defeated by a stone slung at him by David, the future king of Israel. He was said to stand 9 ft. (2.75m) high or, according to another source, 6 ft. (1.8m) high—the difference between a tall story and a tall man.

GIANTS

At the opposite end of the scale from little people are the giants. The idea of giants is probably based on physical reality, since some people are simply very tall. The average height of the Tutsi people of Rwanda/Burundi is 6 ft. (1.8m). The world's tallest man on record is Robert Wadlow, who was 8 ft. 11 in. (2.7m) when he died in 1940. Wadlow was a midget compared to the giants who scare us in mythology—such as Atlas, who held the entire world in his hands; the **Giant of Mont-Saint-Michel** slain by King Arthur; and the **Gigantes**, a race of giants said by the Greeks to be imprisoned inside volcanoes. Our ancestors may have found it more reassuring to believe a volcanic eruption was the work of giants than to think that they were living on a ball of fire. Large natural phenomena such as the **Giant's Causeway**—said to be the ruins of a road built between Ireland and Scotland—were sometimes seen as proof of the existence of giants.

CYCLOPES

Said by legend to be the builders of great prehistoric walls found in parts of Greece and Italy, the Cyclopes were a race of one-eyed giants, thought to enjoy the taste of human flesh. They often featured in the tall tales of seafarers. Ulysses (Odysseus), the mythical king of Ithaca in Greece, and Sinbad the Sailor both reported encounters with them.

GIANT THREATS

Some giants are designed to make people feel small and vulnerable. This huge foot is one piece of what was an enormous statue of the Roman emperor (A.D. 306–337) Constantine the Great. It was built to deliberately extreme proportions to remind people who was in charge.

FRANKENSTEIN & THE LIVING DEAD

VOODOO

Voodoo began in the beliefs of the African slaves of the 1800s who were taken to work on French plantations in the New World. They believed sorcerers had the power to control zombies (the living dead). But zombies weren't really dead at all—they were people who had been fed a soup made of the datura tree. It sedated them, slowing their heart rate, so they only appeared to be dead.

Many religions believe we all have a soul and that the human body is merely a vessel to carry around our consciousness. Myths about the afterlife often start with this question: what happens to someone when they die? The body may stop working, but, so argue the religions, the soul goes somewhere else. A soul without a body is a ghost. So what is a body without a soul?

KURU

Cannibals of the South Pacific used to eat the brains of their enemies in order to gain their powers. Unfortunately, eating human flesh (especially brains) is liable to pass on some terrifying diseases, including kuru, a laughing sickness. The infected person went crazy, supposedly possessed by evil spirits—another version of the living dead. And, once this enemy was defeated, the conquerors would eat his brain and catch the disease, too.

GALVANI'S EXPERIMENTS

In 1791, Italian scientist Luigi Galvani discovered that by passing electricity through the legs of a dead frog, he could make them twitch. It led to the supposition that electricity could bring the dead back to life. Because electricity seemed so mysterious, some people thought it must be the divine force that gave life to dead things.

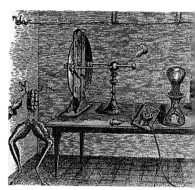

FOOD FOR THOUGHT

There's no arguing with Galvani's experiments. The same process is used to this day to jump-start failed hearts in hospitals. The Frankenstein story is rooted in a fear of science at a time when there were stories of doctors robbing graves so that they could study the corpses. As for the restless dead, see the notes on vampires (pages 36–37). Modern-day afflictions such as schizophrenia and catatonia may have been interpreted in the past as possessions by demons or living deaths. Kuru remains a fascinating topic for the modern scientist. Mad cow disease can pass to humans who have eaten the brains or spinal columns of infected cattle.

DAWN OF THE DEAD

Modern horror movies take the zombie legends of other cultures and put a Christian spin on them. They claim that because hell is full, some souls are waking up back in the bodies that they were supposed to have left behind. Some movies feature the zombies embarking on a quest for human brains—a strange craving that takes its inspiration from the kuru myths.

FRANKENSTEIN'S CREATURE

In Mary Shelley's Gothic novel published in 1818, Frankenstein was the mad professor who made a monster with bits and pieces of several dead bodies sewn together and reanimated with electricity from lightning. But was it human? And if a dead body is reanimated, does it have a soul?

NATURAL MONSTERS

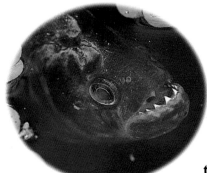

Not all monsters are figments of the human imagination. Perhaps the most fearsome creatures to have lived were the dinosaurs. Fortunately, these prehistoric monsters never shared Earth with us; they died out around 65 million years ago, long before we arrived. But the natural world still has plenty of other fierce creatures to inspire a sense of the monstrous in humankind. The ancestry of some, such as crocodiles, can be traced back to the Mesozoic era when dinosaurs lived. Were we to encounter these creatures roaming free in their natural habitats, the potential dangers facing us would be very real.

KILLER FISH

A piranha school is another monstrous fear. A single fish is ugly but relatively harmless. An entire school of these sharp-toothed creatures can strip the flesh from a creature in the water within seconds. In Brazil in 1981, more than 300 people were eaten alive by piranhas when a boat capsized near Obidos.

FOOD FOR THOUGHT

Are there real-life mammoths in Siberia? The "evidence" has probably come from dead mammoths only recently dug out of ancient ice. In the 1200s, Genghis Khan turned a herd of elephants loose on the Russian steppes. It is unlikely that any of their descendants live undiscovered today, and even less likely is the survival of mammoths.

The ways in which all these creatures are so different to us makes us see them as monstrous. Their teeth, savage speed, and reptilian origins scare us, but they are not monsters. Lions hunt only for food; the crocodile has no interest in human affairs; and no tyrannosaur ever declared war or committed a crime. Only humans have fought to master the natural world. As part of nature, perhaps our greatest fear is that by harming its creatures, we may one day harm ourselves.

TYRANNOSAURUS REX

The most famous of the dinosaurs, this enormous meat-eating predator was genuinely fearsome. Up to 48 ft. (14.5m) long and 20 ft. (6m) high, it weighed almost 8 tons (7 tonnes) and boasted fangs 6 in. (15cm) long. These awesome creatures terrorized East Asia and North America, but luckily for us, the last tyrannosaur died millions of years before the arrival of humanity.

MAMMOTHS

Elephants are large and scary enough as they are. Imagine if they had extra-long tusks and were hairy. The bodies of prehistoric mammoths have been found in the ice of Siberia, and the local tribesmen have been known to take the tusks to sell as ivory. Some people in remote parts of Russia have reported seeing live mammoths, but their stories are difficult to substantiate.

THE KING CHEETAH

Thought for many years to be nothing more than a ghost story, this huge predator with a tigerlike stripe down its back has been known to carry off people along the Mozambique border. Called a *mngwa* by the locals, rumors of its existence were proved true when Paul and Lena Bottriel photographed the "king" cheetah in 1975.

CROCODILE TEARS

Around 2,000 people each year fall prey to saltwater crocodiles. Left over from prehistory, crocodiles have been hunting by the riverside for eons. They are not natural enemies of humans because, in fact, they have been around far longer than the human race. If we invade their natural habitat, it is our own fault if they attack us, yet we have demonized these creatures.

THE LION'S SHARE

Today, lions and tigers are familiar to us from television and zoos. But in the wild, before the days of guns and traps, these big cats were greatly feared. Wise humans left them well alone, even though a lion would attack a human being only if it was provoked. Like many so-called "monsters" of the world, they are more likely to be afraid of us than we are of them.

DRAGONS

SNAKES IN THE GRASS

The serpent is a sign of evil in many cultures. Notice the forked tongue, a symbol of telling lies, and hence of evil and deception.

The dragon is the supermonster of many cultures and is borne of a mixture of many different creatures. The Chinese legend of the birth of the dragon was that as tribes with different animal totems united, they produced a composite creature with the antlers of a deer, the body of a snake, and the wings of a bird (and so on). Eventually, they had invented a creature like no earthly beast.

In Chinese, the word *dragon* is also used to describe waterspouts and tornadoes, which reinforces the idea of a dragon as an unstoppable force of nature. Native Americans created their own equivalent in their "thunder lizard" legends, inspired by their discovery of dinosaur bones—they could not have known that these creatures had been dead for millions of years. Once again, these are examples of the human mind fleshing out monsters created largely in the imagination.

THE EVIL SERPENT

Western dragons have their origins in the Greek *drakon*, meaning "serpent." More likely to be dangerous (Chinese dragons are just powerful), Western dragons have become the personification of evil and of the devil himself (notably, the serpent in the Garden of Eden). Here, Saint George defeats "the dragon." Some other pictures depict the dragon as a human figure.

EARTHQUAKES

On the rare occasions in the past when our ancestors found dinosaur fossils, they did not know how to explain them. Some assumed that the bones were of giant creatures who lived in the bowels of Earth. When one of the sleeping giants shivered, the whole Earth would quake.

THUNDER & LIGHTNING

In China, the word for *dragon* was also used to describe thunder and lightning flashing in the sky. This helps explain the longer snakelike shape of the oriental dragon. To an ancient Chinese sage, this picture would show two dragons fighting in the sky. However, storms weren't the only natural phenomena attributed to the work of dragons. Offshore tornadoes that whisked water into huge whirling spouts were known as sea dragons. This meant that matter-of-fact reports of bad weather could have been misunderstood as attacks by supernatural creatures.

ORIENTAL DRAGONS

East Asian dragons are normally good natured. As long as they are respected, they can act with kindness. According to some stories, a great person may become immortal or a spirit. After many centuries, the spirit becomes a dragonet and dives beneath the earth to sleep. When it finally wakes as a dragon, it tears itself free and flies up to heaven.

A REAL DRAGON

In 1912, a 10-ft. (3-m) lizard that ate pigs and goats was discovered in the islands of the Indian Ocean. It was immediately dubbed the Komodo dragon, as it is still called today. In 1979, an expedition to New Guinea found archaeological evidence of an even bigger lizard. Perhaps a live specimen is still waiting to be discovered.

LAKE MONSTERS

This convincing picture was taken on Loch Ness in 1977. But is it a monster's head or a branch?

Places as far afield as Sweden, Ireland, New Zealand, Africa, and Russia have their own mysterious monsters. In Iceland there is the Lágarfljótsormur, in the North American Lake Champlain there is Champ, and in Canada there is Manipogo, the monster of Lake Winnipeg. Far from being one of a kind, it would seem that Scotland's Loch Ness monster has many cousins around the world.

NESSIE

Ever since A.D. 565, when Saint Columba ordered a creature in the loch to leave humans alone, the Loch Ness monster has been one of the most famous beasts of Scottish folklore. Often presumed to be a throwback to the time of the dinosaurs, Nessie is said to have either a long neck on a large body or to be an eel-like shape, depending on who is telling the story.

Does Nessie have humps? This picture taken in 1951 by Lachlan Stuart would seem to suggest so. Or are they just rocks?

OGOPOGO

In the Canadian province of British Columbia lies Lake Okanagan, where the native Okanagan Indians have always said there was a monster. They called him *Na-ha-ha-itkh* and would throw a meat sacrifice into the lake whenever they crossed it. Known for its humps, snakelike appearance, and thick body, Ogopogo is often sighted but has never harmed anyone in living memory. Ogopogo even had a song written about him in the 1920s: *His mother was an earwig, his father was a whale, a little bit of head, and hardly any tail, and Ogopogo was his name.*

ISSIE

This is a model of Issie, the monster rumored to live in the depths of Lake Ikeda in Japan. Like Nessie, it has never been known to harm humans and seems to be very camera shy. Though many people have *almost* photographed it, a conclusive picture has yet to appear.

LAKE IKEDA, JAPAN

A lake just waiting for a monster.?
This inexplicable ripple could mean
Issie is about to surface.

SEA MONSTERS

TEMPEST

As late as the Elizabethan era (1558–1603), large areas of the globe remained uncharted. When William Shakespeare wrote *The Tempest*, he was inspired by tales of monsters and shipwrecks that had circulated from the New World (the Americas). For the people of premodern times, monsters such as these were thought to lurk just outside mapped areas. Any trip was a trip into the unknown—and into fear.

Two thirds of Earth is covered by water. Although we know most of the land well, there are still unexplored areas of the deep sea that remain a mystery. History is rich with stories of sea monsters. Sailors told tales of many extraordinary creatures such as the now legendary mercreatures who were said to have the body of a human and the tail of a fish. What the sailors saw were probably dolphins, narwhals, or dugongs. Perhaps they had been at sea too long or had taken an extra sip of rum before going on watch. But not all the sightings were quite so fanciful. Until 1938, coelacanths were thought to have become extinct around 50 million years ago. It is now known that a small number of coelacanths live in very deep water off the African coast. If they have survived for millions of years, other prehistoric "monsters," such as the Megalodon, a 100-ft. (30-m) shark, may also still be cruising around in the unexplored depths of some ocean.

FOOD FOR THOUGHT

The thought of a whale shark is very scary, but it isn't a monster. Neither is a shark. We invade their territories, not the other way around. The whales and sharks of ancient tales probably grew over the years to give us the sea monsters from the past, but there's no arguing with some of the evidence. Thirty-ft. (9m) squids have been found and studied by scientists, and if the scars found on sperm whales are anything to go by, they could well be the babies. No one knows how big a full-grown giant squid might be.

FANGTOOTH

This scary-looking fish is actually quite small and is unlikely to show up anywhere near people because it lives miles down in the ocean. On the rare occasions when it is washed up onshore, such teeth might scare humans into imagining what a giant version would look like.

OCTOPUSES

The octopus has always intrigued seafarers. With its eight arms, suckers, and powerful hidden beak, it is one of the strangest creatures of the deep. As stories grow with the telling, many have speculated on the existence of giant octopuses large enough to swallow a human whole.

GIANT SQUID

Thought to be the stuff of legend, the giant squid (or kraken) may actually exist. The first people to discuss it were the crews of whaling ships in the 1800s. Some whales they killed had the scars of giant suckers on them, as if they had survived a battle. F. T. Bullen reported a harpooned sperm whale vomiting thousands of squids (its traditional diet). Also among the debris were huge pieces of tentacles as thick as a man's body. This 19th-century Japanese print (left) shows a giant squid as one of the legendary Dragon King's faithful army.

WHALES

The great size of whales has always struck dread into the hearts of sailors, but these peaceful creatures have no interest in harming humanity. Their value as food and for raw materials in candles and corsets (among other things) meant that they have been hunted to the brink of extinction. But whales must have been terrifying for early whalers who had nothing but spears to throw.

SHARKS

Sharks are our modern-day sea monsters, but not because they are evil (although, like this blue shark, some do look menacing). Unless provoked, most sharks will leave humans alone. The biggest-known fish in the world is the whale shark—at a huge 60 ft. (18m) long—but it doesn't eat people, just tiny plant and animal organisms called plankton.

WERECREATURES

A FULL MOON

Werewolves supposedly take on their beastly shape during a full moon, when supernatural powers are at their greatest.

A true werecreature is half man, half beast. From early prehistoric cave paintings we can see that primitive shamans were thought to have the power of shape shifting. Similar stories were told of the Vikings, who often wore wolf skins to strike fear into their enemies. In modern mythology, such as the movie *I Was a Teenage Werewolf*, werewolves have been given an additional dimension: the teenage boy's monstrous fear of never being loved, of having a dark side that cannot be tamed, and of being a rebel without a cause—or a beast in search of a beauty to tame him.

FOOD FOR THOUGHT

The idea of changing into a wolf (or in some cultures into tigers, bears, or lions) shows a natural human fear of the monstrous. It symbolizes leaving the safety of civilization and plunging back into the past to become the very thing our ancestors sought to hide from—our own animal nature. As with the shape-shifting vampire, some people may have been malevolently motivated to blame the random attack of a wild animal on an enemy disguised as a monster. The pictures here are not of werewolves—they're just ordinary wolves! And someday we'll wake up and notice that the better-lit nights of the full moon make it easier for humans to commit nocturnal crimes, especially in the past when there were no streetlights.

THE WOLF OF THE WILD

Humankind has always had an uneasy relationship with the wolf. At some time in the distant past, a branch of the wolf family became "man's best friend," but wolves, closely related to dogs, have remained fierce creatures. Although they are feared for hunting in packs, they do not attack humans unless provoked by them.

THE FRENCH WOLF

Thought to be a werewolf, the Beast of Gévaudan terrorized the French countryside for three years between 1764 and 1767. Said to be the size of a cow, it claimed the lives of more than 60 peasants by the time it was killed—shot in the chest by a silver bullet. Its stomach was said to contain the collarbone of a young woman, but its carcass was buried and has never been found.

ANCIENT WOLVES

Ancient writers talked of lycanthropy, kuanthropy, and boanthropy, conditions of insanity in which afflicted persons believed themselves to be a wolf, a dog, or a cow. In Northern Europe, similar tales were told of men who turned into bears and, in Africa, hyenas. Greek historian Herodotus (c. 480–425 B.C.) claimed the Neuri people of Sarmatia (northeast Europe) were sorcerers: "For each Neurian changes himself once a year into the form of a wolf and continues in that form for several days, after which he resumes his former shape."

BEAUTY & THE BEAST

The tale of a man who looks (and often behaves) like an animal is not limited to werewolves. It also crops up in *The Strange Case of Dr. Jekyll and Mr Hyde* (1886) by Robert Louis Stevenson and in the fairy tale *Beauty and the Beast*. The stories tell of savage creatures who menace beautiful girls—timeless representations of mistrust between men and women.

HAIRY MEN OF MANDALAY

Don't believe humans can get that hairy? A disease called hypertrichosis can cause excessive facial hair, as in this photograph of hairy men from Mandalay in Burma (now Myanmar). Since our distant ape ancestors had hair all over, it is only relatively recently in human history that we began to lose our all-over fur.

THE YETI

The abominable snowman, or yeti, is perhaps the most famous apelike creature. It may be a distant apelike relative of humans. The people of the Himalaya Mountains of south-central Asia believe it exists, and the mountain range is so remote that it is possible that undiscovered creatures do live there. In 1975, a Polish hiker named Janusz Tomaszczuk claimed he had been approached by an apelike creature in the Himalayas. His screams drove it away.

THE SCOTTISH SNOWMAN

This photograph was taken high up on Ben Nevis, the highest mountain in the British Isles. Is it the Scottish equivalent of the yeti? Or just a man in a gorilla suit?

YETI'S FOOTPRINTS

Nobody has ever captured a yeti, but its footprints have been photographed. These deep, large footprints are spaced wide apart and suggest a tall, heavy creature. It certainly isn't human. But it might be the elusive Tibetan blue bear, a creature that has not been seen alive by Westerners but whose skins have been sold to museums.

GREAT APES

Like the werewolf, what scares us most about the great apes is how alike, and yet how different, they are to us. The gentlest of the great apes, the mountain gorilla was regarded as a fanciful invention of storytellers until the early years of the 1900s. Perhaps the stories of the Himalayan yeti, the American Bigfoot, or the Russian Alma are equally well founded.

KING KONG

A classic horror movie tells the tale of King Kong, a 50-ft. (15-m) prehistoric great ape who is captured, taken to New York City, and put on display. He escapes and terrorizes the city before finally falling to his death from the Empire State Building. His climactic rampage through the city was the result of human intervention, which made his death all the more tragic.

BIG FEET

If this 1995 Bigfoot photograph is a fake, it means that someone has been crazy enough to make false Bigfoot tracks running for several miles in remote parts of the U.S. and Canada.

BIGFOOT

In 1967, Roger Patterson took this famous film of an apelike figure in northern California. Its height is estimated at 6 ft. 5 in. (2m). Could *Pithecanthropus erectus*, a species of primitive human believed to be extinct, still live in remote parts of the world?

FOOD FOR THOUGHT

There may yet be more creatures for us to discover in the wilderness. The existence of a Scottish ape-man is doubtful, but Canada and the Himalayas are large enough to allow for the possibility of undiscovered life. Since mountain gorillas exist, there's a chance that the yeti could, too. Or perhaps Bigfoot? Both these great apes are reputed to live in wastelands devoid of human habitation and would probably be more scared of us than we are of them.

SCARING YOUR ENEMIES

This suit of Japanese samurai armor is designed to look monstrous. In the heat of battle, warriors needed all the help they could get. Horned helmets or even spiked armor for their horses all helped terrify their enemies.

GRENDEL

In the Old English epic tale *Beowulf*, Grendel was the troll-like creature who plagued King Hrothgar's hall for 12 years. Eventually, Grendel was slain by Beowulf, the hero who wrestled with him and tore off his arm. Grendel's mother came seeking vengeance for her son and proved to be an even more dangerous enemy.

FAMILY FORTUNES

In the Middle Ages, few people could read and write. Noble families and public figures therefore needed a recognizable mark to symbolize and display their power. The family's mark was made into a seal to authenticate legal documents and was also used on buildings, flags, and armor. These marks often included powerful beasts such as lions and bears. Noble families joined in the same way as prehistoric tribes. This combination meant new heraldic beasts had to be created that included different parts from each family's coat of arms. These new nonexistent creatures became symbols of larger, more powerful families.

GRIFFIN

The griffin is part eagle, part lion. These two heraldic symbols are signs of power and strength—and combined, they make a truly scary monster. A remarkably similar idea of something superpowerful is found in Chinese culture—a tiger with wings.

HERALDIC BEASTS

Noble families often regarded their family symbols as guardian spirits, or designed them to strike fear into their enemies.

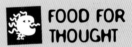

CHIMERA

In Greek mythology, this fire-breathing monster had the body of a lion, a goat's head emerging from its back, and a serpent's tail. A fearsome creature, its origin can be traced to the geography around the Chimaera volcano in Lycia, an ancient region on the coast of southwest Asia Minor. It had a fiery summit, lions in its upper forests, goats on the lower slopes, and serpents in the marshes at its foot.

FOOD FOR THOUGHT

Was Grendel a real person? Probably not, but as a symbol of an enemy tribe, he must have seemed a fearsome enemy. Many of these heraldic monsters are symbols of synergy, of the power gained through cooperation with others. They embody the challenge "You and whose army?"—a clear threat to your enemies that if they cross you, they also cross your allies. The concept of mixed breeds still scares us. Just look at the horror story "The Fly" in which a laboratory accident forces a man and a fly to become one fearsome creature. Modern-day horror stories of genetic mutation and experiments continue to inspire monstrous stories.

THE BERMUDA TRIANGLE

In 1945, five Avenger bomber planes took off from Fort Lauderdale, Florida, and disappeared without a trace near Bermuda, a small island in the Atlantic Ocean. The boat sent to search for them also vanished. Since then, hundreds of other ships and airplanes have disappeared in the same triangle of sea. Explanations have included alien abduction, sea monsters, and unusual magnetic forces. A magnetic storm could have caused intruments to fail or lost pilots may have run out of fuel.

FOOD FOR THOUGHT

The law of probability suggests that out of a huge number of predictions, some of them are bound to come true. Those that don't are quickly forgotten. The same law can be applied to the Bermuda Triangle. In any area of 250,000 sq. mi. (647,500km²), disappearances are not uncommon, and the Bermuda Triangle is an area of extreme weather conditions. Probability could also be a factor in the curse of Tutankhamen—opening a tomb sealed for more than 3,000 years could release unknown airborne bacteria. However, people have an appetite for myths, and today, the Internet spreads and embellishes modern myths much more quickly than has ever before been possible. If they are appealing and plausible enough, myths will spread, whether or not there is any real evidence to support them.

MYSTERY, MYTH, & PROPHECY

It is human nature to endeavor to understand the nature of what happens around us. Until we understand unexplained events, we cannot make informed choices about how to react to them. Myths usually start after something incredible has happened for which there seems no rational explanation. As science advances, more is understood about the world and how it works. Nevertheless, many mysteries endure. Strange events occur every day, and because it takes time to make sense of them, myths can sometimes grow to epic proportions. Mysteries, like our belief in psychic phenomena, are complex to unravel since they involve the nature of belief itself.

THE CURSE OF TUTANKHAMEN

In 1922, the tomb of Pharaoh Tutankhamen (1336–1327 B.C.) was discovered by Howard Carter, an archaeologist working for Lord George Carnarvon. It is rumored that Carter destroyed an inscription in the tomb that read: *Death will slay with his wings whoever disturbs the pharaoh's peace.* A legacy of death did seem to follow the excavation. Lord Carnarvon died in 1923, at the age of 57. Then an archaeologist, an American financier, and a British industrialist all died after visiting the tomb. During the next seven years, 22 more people connected with the discovery also died, many in unusual circumstances. However, Carter himself lived another 17 years and died at the age of 65.

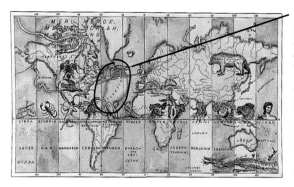

LOST BENEATH THE WAVES

The lost island of Atlantis was said to have been the center of a highly advanced civilization. According to ancient legends, Atlantean scientists understood the human mind and were great magicians. Atlantis was said to have been destroyed by a simultaneous volcanic eruption, earthquake, and tidal wave, but some Atlanteans escaped and preserved their magical arts. No convincing geological or archaeological evidence has ever been found.

TITANIC DISASTER

Extraordinarily, some disasters are foretold. Predictions can be recorded before an event, which may seem to prove an ability to foretell the future. Before major disasters, such as the sinking of the *Titanic*, the calamity is often predicted, sometimes with detailed accounts of what will occur. One theory is that disasters involve so many deaths that they create an energy that can be felt by sensitive psychics. This cannot be proven, although many people who do not consider themselves psychic also experience premonitions of danger.

NOSTRADAMUS & PROPHECIES

Nostradamus was a French doctor known for his treatment of plague in the 1500s. In 1555, he published a book of obscure prophecies in the form of quatrains (poems of four lines). His followers believe that he predicted various important events that happened hundreds of years later, but his prophecies are so vague that it is difficult to match them to specific incidents. This prophecy was interpreted as foretelling the 1945 bombing of Hiroshima and Nagasaki in Japan: *Near the harbor and in two cities will be two scourges, the likes of which have never been seen. Hunger, plague within, people thrown out by the sword will cry for help from the great immortal God.*

ECTOPLASM

This medium is emitting ectoplasm. Ectoplasm allegedly is a substance called up out of a medium's body to give a spirit physical reality. Silvery white in color, it resembles thin fabric and forms the body and clothes of a spirit while it is communicating. Touching a spirit formed of ectoplasm is said to cause the medium to become sick. Although it hasn't been proved that all mediums fake ectoplasm, it is possible to swallow a skein of cotton and gradually regurgitate it.

REST IN PEACE?

The words *Rest in Peace* carved on gravestones imply that the dead might not necessarily rest or be at peace. Over the centuries, many stories have evolved about ghosts who do not rest. They haunt people or places for revenge or because they have left something undone in their lives. Some people have reported that they live comfortably with supernatural neighbors. Others say ghosts are dangerous and can smash objects, make eerie noises, and create a perceptible aura of menace in a house.

CLAIRVOYANTS & MEDIUMS

Clairvoyancy is one of the earliest documented psychic phenomena and one of the most lucrative for hoaxers. Clairvoyants and mediums claim that, through them, we can contact the spirit of a dead person. Some mediums claim to be able to only speak to these spirits, while others claim they can give the spirits a physical form. Mediums have often been exposed as hoaxers or have admitted to defrauding their clients. A grieving person's fervent wish to contact a dead person they love makes them susceptible to such hoaxes. Although many mediums have undoubtedly claimed abilities that they do not possess, clairvoyancy has yet to be fully investigated.

QUESTIONING THE SPIRITS

It may seem strange today, but in ancient times, it was common to ask spirits for advice. Oracles were visionaries who went into a trance to ask questions on behalf of seekers. One of the most famous was Pythia, the oracle at Delphi in Greece. She used volcanic fumes and drugs to assist her visions. Although ancient and modern mediums have posed many questions to spirits and entered into long conversations with some of them, no real answers have ever been obtained about life after death or that prove the existence of spirits.

CONTACTING THE DEAD

To contact the spirits, mediums hold a séance. A group of people who wish to speak to a dead person, or perhaps ask about the afterlife, form a circle around a table and hold hands while the medium attempts to summon the presence of a spirit. Mediums have been known to fake the responses of spirits by using devices that strike the underside of the table in order to produce ghostly knocks in reply to questions. However, some mediums have produced inexplicable effects under test conditions designed by scientists attempting to expose them as frauds.

THE CASE OF KATIE KING

One famous medium was investigated by Victorian scientist William Crookes. Florence Cook claimed she could manifest the spirit of Katie King (right), who appeared at séances and talked to guests. Florence was suspected of dressing up as the spirit herself or of having an accomplice do so. Crookes asserted that his investigation had convinced him of the spirit's existence. Crookes didn't publish his findings in any scientific journals, but he never retracted his claims. Later, it was alleged that he had helped in the medium's fraud in order to have an affair with her.

FOOD FOR THOUGHT

If there is life after death, it would seem reasonable for dead spirits to want to contact the living. Ghosts might be trying to draw attention to the identity of their killer or to where they buried the family silver. Spirits contacted by mediums might want their relatives to know they are happy and at peace. Some mediums are fakes who take advantage of people who are vulnerable after the death of a loved one. In their own defense, mediums might say they are trying only to provide comfort to the bereaved. And just because some are fakes, it doesn't prove they all are. Some mediums could be genuine.

SPIRITS & SPIRITUALISM

People who claim to possess psychic abilities often believe in the existence of spirits—nonphysical beings who are thought to be gods or the souls of the dead. Some claim they can contact spirits using psychic powers. Spirits can be benevolent, guiding or teaching the humans they care about. But some malicious spirits are believed to return to the physical world to deliberately cause harm. Some spirits are tricksters; amused by the antics of mortals, they play jokes on people who attempt to contact them. Even among spiritualists and practitioners of magic who believe in the existence of spirits, there is no consistent theory about what they are or what methods should be used to communicate with them.

SPIRIT GUIDES

Shamans, like other types of magicians, use spirit guides as aids and symbols in their magic. Brazilian shamans believe people have spirits shaped like different animals, the most powerful of which is the jaguar. Native American shamanism involves attuning magic to the paths of different animals. A wolf shaman is expected to be tireless and fierce, while a coyote shaman is a devious trickster. Spirit guides are not necessarily animals. In shamanic magic, strong images and physical symbols are important. The greater the belief in a symbol, the greater its power.

REINCARNATION

Many people believe that after death our soul is reincarnated (reborn) in another body. Buddhists believe that good or evil deeds in one life will be rewarded or punished in the next. Hindus believe a human who leads an evil life may be reincarnated as an animal. Those who lead worthy lives attain ever-higher levels of enlightenment in each life until they pass on to the next stage of existence. Regression hypnotists have put people into a trancelike state in which they apparently recall events from their previous lives. Some people have even spoken languages that they do not know in their present lives. However, it is difficult to prove or disprove the existence of reincarnation.

FOOD FOR THOUGHT

Belief in the survival of the soul or spirit after death has been widespread throughout human history. It seems unbearable to think that we and the people we love will stop existing when we die. And if we do have a spirit that exists independently of our body, why should other living things not have one as well?

BODY & SOUL

The ancient Egyptians believed that in addition to the senses of the body, a person is divided into many different spiritual parts. Egyptian myths tell of great magicians who could separate their *ka* (soul or spirit double) from their body and make it fly in the form of a bird. Spells played an important part in the everyday lives of the Egyptians. They believed that all words have power and used them to bring about desired events or to curse their enemies.

DREAMTIME

Aboriginal Australians have a complex set of beliefs about the supernatural powers of their ancestors and the Dreamtime in which they created everything that now exists. As depicted in their rock paintings and artifacts, they see the natural world as a powerful and mysterious place, with no distinction between the commonplace and the supernatural. They regard both as essential aspects of life.

SHAMANISM & WITCH DOCTORS

Today, shamans, like this one from Nigeria, still watch over their peoples in Africa, South America, the Far East, and the U.S. among its Native Americans. A tribal shaman (witch doctor) is a magician and healer who cares for the bodies and souls of his people. He is as likely to be asked to hunt for a missing soul stolen by an enemy as a cure for an illness. Shamanism is often passed on through families of witches. After their death, they are believed to continue as guardian spirits of their tribe.

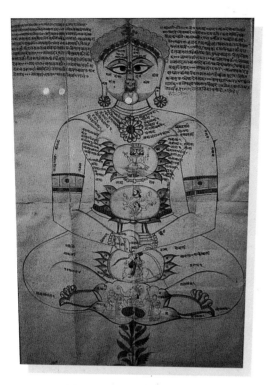

MAGIC ENERGIES, PSYCHIC POWERS

Different belief systems have evolved around occult powers. Some beliefs involve worship and include psychic phenomena as aspects of religious activity. Some people believe that paranormal powers are part of normal life and try to live according to complex rituals. Others fear any manifestation of the supernatural and try to ignore any evidence of, or reference, to it. Our fascination with the paranormal ensures that we will continue to investigate and attempt to understand supernatural abilities and events that do not conform to our existing ideas about the world.

CHAKRA POINTS

Chakra is the Hindu word to describe one of the main centers of spiritual power in the human body—points along the spine where energy is believed to be transformed into a usable form. Raw energy is said to be drawn from the earth and fed into the chakra points. There are seven principle chakras in the body, and detailed maps of each chakra and their connecting meridians and pathways have been used in Eastern mysticism and medicine for thousands of years.

LEGENDARY TREASURES

Similar to the balance of the elements (earth, fire, air, and water) is the traditional pagan belief in four legendary items of great power. In mythology, these treasures are usually a sword, a spear, a cup, and a stone. Each has different powers and stories attached to it. Pagan legends tell of the cauldron of Dagda, a cup of plenty said to provide a never-ending supply of food. The four objects are also symbols in the tarot, a deck of cards used in fortunetelling. Magical items feature throughout history. During World War II, Adolf Hitler collected such objects, believing they would make him invincible.

RITUAL PAINTINGS

The life of the Navajo Indians, a Native American people who live in Arizona, New Mexico, and Utah, involves close attention to rituals and magical rites. The Navajo live in harmony with the environment and carry out their daily activities with customs and chants intended to bring good fortune and to ward off evil. One of their most impressive rituals is the curing ceremony, presided over by a medicine man (a sorcerer who tends to the spiritual well-being of a tribe). It involves drawing elaborate paintings in sand, which they believe help cure illness. Rather than magic, perhaps such rituals help focus the mind. Believing they'll work may be enough to make them do so.

CHI ENERGY

The Chinese discipline of chi is used in acupuncture and in the martial art tai chi. Chi is the energy that exists in all living things. This belief also exists in other cultures and religions. The yin-yang in Taoism symbolizes the two opposite and complementary forces of cosmic energy. Yin is feminine and negatively charged; yang is male and positively charged. Each contains part of the other, as seen in the yin-yang symbol at the center of this picture of three tai chi sages. It is possible that a master of chi can imbue an object with more chi. Uncharacteristically, Sony Corporation funded a seven-year project researching psychic phenomena. The tests included a chi practitioner attempting to project chi energy into one of two glasses of water. A second chi practitioner then tried to identify the glass with more chi energy. These tests are said to have had a 70 percent success rate, but the test conditions and controls have not been verified.

 FOOD FOR THOUGHT

Well-established magical systems, such as chi, can be as clearly thought out and consistent as conventional scientific knowledge. In China, for example, acupuncture (a treatment based on the chi system) has been accepted as scientifically valid for hundreds of years. It took a long time for Western doctors to take it seriously as a medical treatment. Other healing systems could offer the same.

BLOOD MAGIC

One belief common to different types of practicing magicians concerns the power of blood. Black magic ceremonies, voodoo, and African shamanism all include rites that involve sacrificing animals, usually a black rooster or a goat, although other animals may be used.

MADMAN OR MAGICIAN?

Grigori Rasputin (c. 1871–1916) was a Siberian monk whose reputation discredited the field of psychic research in Russia for many years. He was politically ambitious and gained considerable power at the court of Nicholas II, the last czar of Russia (1868–1918). Rasputin claimed his supernatural powers could cure Alexei, the czar's only son, of hemophilia—a blood-clotting disorder. He succeeded in convincing the czarina of his abilities, and her patronage of Rasputin helped bring the royal family into disrepute. Rasputin was eventually assassinated by nobles jealous of his influence.

GRAND MASTER OF THE GOLDEN DAWN

Aleister Crowley (1875–1947) wanted to be known as "the wickedest man alive." He became grand master of the Golden Dawn, a secret magic society, but was expelled for extreme practices. He eventually believed he was a vampire and used a bewildering variety of drugs to enhance his magical powers. He attracted many disciples during and after his lifetime and once said, "I may be a black magician, but I'm a bloody great one."

CONJURING TRICKS

Harry Houdini was an escapologist and conjurer who counterfeited psychic abilities onstage. He was interested in spiritualism and published a book entitled *A Magician Among the Spirits* in an attempt to discredit mediums. Because Houdini knew how to fake psychic powers, he didn't believe they actually existed.

CONJURERS OR MAGICIANS?

Paranormal phenomena and psychic powers are often faked by conjurers who develop techniques to entertain or deceive their credulous audiences. Some stage magicians admit freely that their feats, such as mind reading and levitation, are tricks, while others claim their abilities are genuine. Magicians such as Aleister Crowley and Grigori Rasputin managed to convince themselves and other people that their psychic talents were real. But their authenticity is doubted because of the money and sense of power that such magicians gain from their activities.

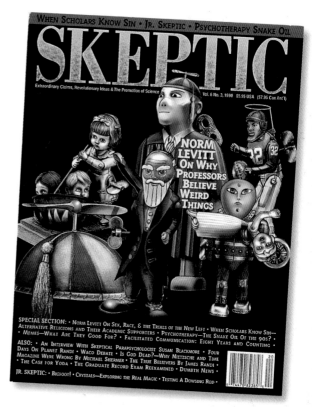

WHEN SCHOLARS KNOW SIN • JR. SKEPTIC • PSYCHOTHERAPY SNAKE OIL

SKEPTIC

Extraordinary Claims, Revolutionary Ideas & The Promotion of Science

Vol. 6 No. 3, 1998 $5.95 USA ($7.95 Can /Int'l)

NORM LEVITT ON WHY PROFESSORS BELIEVE WEIRD THINGS

SPECIAL SECTION: • NORM LEVITT ON SEX, RACE, & THE TRIALS OF THE NEW LEFT • WHEN SCHOLARS KNOW SIN—ALTERNATIVE RELIGIONS AND THEIR ACADEMIC SUPPORTERS • PSYCHOTHERAPY—THE SNAKE OIL OF THE 90S? • MEMES—WHAT ARE THEY GOOD FOR? • FACILITATED COMMUNICATION: EIGHT YEARS AND COUNTING •
ALSO: • AN INTERVIEW WITH SKEPTICAL PARAPSYCHOLOGIST SUSAN BLACKMORE • FOUR DAYS ON PLANET RANDI • WACO DEBATE • IS GOD DEAD?—WHY NIETZSCHE AND TIME MAGAZINE WERE WRONG BY MICHAEL SHERMER • THE TRUE BELIEVERS BY JAMES RANDI • THE CASE FOR YODA • THE GRADUATE RECORD EXAM REEXAMINED • DUMBTH NEWS •
JR. SKEPTIC: • BIGFOOT! • CRYSTALS—EXPLORING THE REAL MAGIC • TESTING A DOWSING ROD •

PROFESSIONAL SKEPTICS

A skeptic always doubts and questions accepted beliefs and mistrusts new theories and ideas until they are scientifically proven, and even then tends to think nothing is certain. *Skeptic* magazine attempts to refute beliefs that, in its opinion, are "180 degrees out of phase with reason."

THE POWER OF THE MIND

Uri Geller is an Israeli-British stage magician who claims to use the power of his mind to bend metal objects, restart watches, and force computers to malfunction. He has performed these feats and others under strict test conditions but has also been exposed as a fake by people who claim to have seen him falsifying his demonstrations. Since Uri Geller originally was an amateur conjurer, people tend to doubt his psychic abilities. The phenomenon of metal bending is not unique to Geller. It has been studied in others who claim to possess a similar power, as well as replicated by metallurgists (experts in metals and their properties).

FOOD FOR THOUGHT

It is impossible to prove that a conjurer does not have magical powers. It may be possible to reproduce the same results by nonmagical means, but that is not the same. Not many people really believe stage magicians have genuine magical powers, but it is more fun to suspend disbelief and enjoy the show. The ingenuity with which some conjuring tricks are devised—levitating, or making a railroad car disappear—is often more impressive than if magic were actually being used.

MYSTICISM & MIRACLES

The psychic powers sometimes attributed to prophets and mystics may be believed in religious contexts, but their existence has not been scientifically proven. Every major religion has accounts of miracles performed by priests and saints who possessed unusual and powerful abilities. Religious believers claim their god or gods bestow such powers on their followers in times of crisis. The evidence for the existence of miracles is difficult to trust because "miraculous" events can be faked. However, the evidence is just as difficult to disprove because we understand so little about psychic phenomena.

THE SHROUD OF TURIN

First displayed in 1353, the Shroud of Turin, which has the image of a crucified man imprinted on it, was said to be the burial sheet of Jesus Christ. In 1989, carbon-dating techniques were used to determine its age. Now generally accepted, the results dated the shroud between A.D. 1260 and 1390—centuries later than Christ's crucifixion. However, there have been allegations that anticlerical scientists faked the carbon-dating tests, and the shroud is still venerated as a holy relic.

STIGMATA

A well-documented religious phenomenon, stigmata are the five wounds left on Jesus Christ after he was nailed to the cross. Since the crucifixion, similar wounds have appeared spontaneously on certain people such as Antonio Ruffini (right). They are generally passionate Christians but have nothing else in common. Stigmata do not seem to be caused by disease or self-inflicted injury. Some people's wounds last for years, while others heal quickly. Today, stigmata remain a scientific mystery and are considered by the Roman Catholic Church to be a miracle.

HEALING POWERS

Certain religious statues and paintings are believed to have miraculous powers, capable of healing people of minor and even terminal illnesses. Every year, thousands of people make pilgrimages to religious sites, and for many of them, it is their last hope of becoming well. These "cures" often have an immediate beneficial effect, but it has yet to be proved that they make long-term improvements to health. One such statue said to possess the power to heal is the Madonna in Lourdes, France (left).

THE RESURRECTION OF CHRIST

Common to many religions, resurrection is one of the most impressive of alleged miracles. Skeptics who don't believe in divine miracles, or followers of different religious beliefs, sometimes claim that the prophets and demigods of ancient religions were people with powerful psychic powers.

FAKIRS

Indian fakirs enter a trancelike state in order to perform astounding feats of endurance. In 1835, the maharajah of Lahore asked a fakir named Haridas to demonstrate his abilities. Haridas was buried underground in a padlocked coffin with barley sown in the soil above it. Forty days later, Haridas was exhumed alive and well. He was never found to have cheated. Fakirs still give displays of their powers, which include lying unhurt on a bed of nails, walking on hot coals, and levitation. Although these psychic phenomena have been well documented, scientists are still trying to figure out how some of them are done.

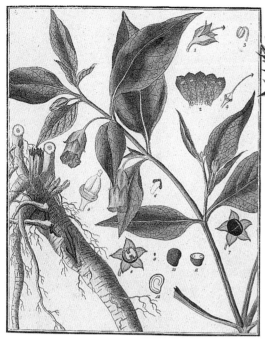

BLACK HATS & BROOMSTICKS

Women who are believed to have magic powers are called witches. According to folklore, witches wear black, ride a broomstick, brew magic potions in a cauldron, and have a familiar (spirit helper), often in the form of a cat. If any of this were true, witches would be very easy to identify. In the past, many women were persecuted for being witches just because they lived alone or used herbs to cure illnesses. The old superstitions inspired many fictional characters in fairy tales and other literature such as Shakespeare's play *Macbeth*.

DEADLY NIGHTSHADE

When consumed or smoked, some plants have properties that cause people to have fearful visions or strange sensations.

Belladonna (deadly nightshade), a poisonous herb, was often used in magical rites. It can cause the hallucination of flying, which may be why some people believed they were witches and confessed to having flown by magical means.

🥠 FOOD FOR THOUGHT

Author Arthur C. Clarke wrote, "Any sufficiently advanced technology is indistinguishable from magic." Many of the things we take for granted—such as radios, computers, and airplanes—would have seemed magical to our ancestors. It is human nature to look for explanations for what we do not understand, and "magic" can be used to explain almost anything. It may be that there are new sciences not currently known to us, which could explain some of these phenomena. And perhaps the idea of magic is more attractive to us because we have no explanation for it.

THE COURT MAGICIAN

An English scholar, Dr. John Dee (1527–1608) was a mathematician and astrologer who studied sorcery and practiced as a magician at various European courts. He claimed angels had taught him magic spells and Enoch, the language that Adam supposedly spoke in the Garden of Eden. Queen Elizabeth I chose January 14 for her coronation because Dr. Dee told her that date was astrologically fortunate. A black obsidian mirror, which he said had been given to him by an angel, can still be seen at the British Museum in London, England.

WITCHES & WARLOCKS

When events and our sense of things seem beyond understanding, humankind has tended to attribute them to the existence of psychic abilities or supernatural powers. Such beliefs are often found underlying religions, superstitions, and mysteries. All through the 1900s, scientists have sought explanations for a variety of psychic phenomena, but there remains much to discover and understand. To unravel their mysteries and evaluate the evidence, we must first explore the history of beliefs in the paranormal.

MAGIC OF THE GODS

The priests and priestesses of ancient religions used magical rites in their ceremonies. Gods such as the Egyptian Isis (above) and the Persian Mithras had mysteries into which only their followers were initiated. Becoming one with the god was the main aspiration. Isis was a goddess of love, death, cunning, and magic. Hieroglyphs and magical inscriptions adorned her temples. Because *Isis* means "wisdom," her supporters were expected to be intelligent and reasoning. Plutarch, an ancient Greek philosopher, described Isis worshipers as seekers of the hidden truths behind the gods.

A DEMONIC PACT

Witches and warlocks were suspected of being in league with the devil, who gave them magical powers in return for their souls. Anyone who claimed they could do magic was therefore believed to be unholy. English dramatist Christopher Marlowe (1564–1593) and German poet Johann Wolfgang von Goethe (1749–1832) both wrote plays about Johann Faust (1480–1538), a legendary German magician who sold his soul in return for increased knowledge. From within the protection of a ritual circle, Dr. Faust is shown here summoning Mephistopheles, an agent of the devil.

WARDS AGAINST EVIL

Many customs and superstitions are based on magic. Most of them are designed to ward off evil influences, but they also often ascribe magical powers to certain items. For example, a horseshoe hung over a doorway is thought to prevent witches from entering.

BLACK & WHITE MAGIC

Magic practices traditionally fall into one of two categories. Black magic includes magical rites that make use of blood, death, and the name of the devil. White magic encompasses powers of healing, visions, and some religious ceremonies. Some people practice magic today but, in most cases, without the rituals and formulas used in the past. Not all practitioners of magic think of themselves as either black or white magicians. Some consider the study of magic to be a science that can be used for either good or evil purposes. Others deliberately choose to study only white or black magic.

FOOD FOR THOUGHT

Witchcraft used to be a convenient excuse for misfortune. If a cow got sick or a field was blighted, it was easier to blame an old woman who lived alone rather than accept that you had been unlucky, or even that you had not cared for the cow or field properly. Fear of witchcraft spread quickly, and anyone who did not join in the condemnation of witches might have been accused of being one. This led to witch trials such as those in Salem, Massachusetts, in 1692, when more than 150 people from one village were arrested in antiwitchcraft hysteria. In 17th-century Europe, even a birthmark could brand you as a witch, and 40,000 people were executed in Great Britain alone—a small fraction of the total in Europe as a whole.

CRYSTAL HEALING

It is a long-held belief that crystals and semiprecious stones have magical healing properties. In ancient Egypt, magicians sometimes advised people to eat the powdered remains of magical amulets to cure illnesses. This belief is still popular today, with crystal healers claiming they can cure minor illnesses. Some even say that crystals are effective against more dangerous diseases. A crystal is usually placed against the skin of a patient, but sometimes it is powdered and ingested.

DEVIL WORSHIP

Witches and black magicians who made pacts with the devil held ceremonies to worship him. The Black Mass was a corruption of Christian worship designed to summon the devil and typically involved acts of deliberate evil designed to please him. The Witches' Sabbath was a midnight ritual in which witches and demons danced around a fire. The tradition is probably connected to older Celtic festivals held on Walpurgis Night and Halloween. Although the Witches' Sabbath is still held today, it is not necessarily with the intent to summon the devil. It can also be held as a celebration of birth and new life.

SOLOMON THE MAGICIAN

In the A.D. 900s, King Solomon of Israel was said to be a great magician. The *Key of Solomon*, one of the oldest-known books of spells, tells how he "discovered the secret of how to shut a million satanic spirits in a bottle of black glass, together with 72 of their kings." The book was used by black magicians because it also told how to make a pact with the devil, summon spirits, gain fortunes, and extend life. Solomon's seal (two interlocked triangles, left) is often used in magic rites.

VOODOO

Voodoo is a religious cult practiced in parts of Africa, South America, and the Caribbean. It evolved as a combination of Catholicism and West African traditions on 17th-century slave plantations. Voodoo followers believe that while in a trance, a person can be beneficially possessed by their ancestors or gods. However, it also has a dark side when used in black magic. Voodoo sorcerers claim they can create zombies—people raised from the dead who are subject to the will of the sorcerer and who obey his commands. Voodoo dolls are made by sorcerers using hair or nail clippings of a living individual. Sticking pins into a doll is believed to harm the person it represents.

BOARD GAMES

Originally called the planchette, Ouija dates from the 1850s and is a triangular board supported by two wheels and a pencil. The pressure of hands placed on the surface moves the board, and the pencil writes messages (apparently from the spirits) on a piece of paper beneath it. In 1868, American toy companies copied and refined the idea to include the letters of the alphabet and the words *yes* and *no*. The planchette then had to move only from letter to letter to spell out its message. A Ouija board is a popular way of contacting spirits during a séance, although the messages can easily be faked by players controlling the planchette.

RECEPTIVE MINDS

Meditation is a technique of clearing the mind. Many psychic practitioners use it to prepare their minds to be receptive to telepathic thoughts or messages from the spirit world. Meditation is also used in prayer, in healing, and as a relaxation technique. Prolonged meditation induces a trancelike state in which all the capabilities of the mind are concentrated on a single thought. Yoga is an Asian meditative technique that has become increasingly popular in the West.

MUSIC FROM THE GRAVE

Some mediums specialize in contacting the spirits of celebrities. Rosemary Brown, a housewife in London, England, claimed she had been contacted by the spirits of many eminent composers such as Beethoven, who dictated musical scores to her. Experts have said her work was more than just imitation, but Rosemary's lack of musical training means she had been able to retrieve only fragments. Another medium, Stella Horrocks, produces entire novels that she claims have been dictated to her by dead authors such as Jane Austen. She goes into a trance to write, and the handwriting for each novelist is different.

EXORCISM

Some branches of the Christian Church still perform exorcisms. These rituals are intended not to summon spirits but to dispel them. In the Bible, exorcisms are performed to cast out demons who have possessed a person's body. Nowadays, exorcism is used to dispel ghosts or spirits. An exorcist commands the possessing spirit to depart using the name of God to enforce his injunction. Exorcism, like a powerful spell, requires three items for the ritual—a bible, a bell, and a candle.

CHANNELING THE SUPERNATURAL

Many psychics and mediums believe the spirit world can be channeled and used in order to put people in touch with their own unconscious minds. Some psychics believe that people leave images of themselves wherever they have been. Police have occasionally hired psychics to help catch criminals, identifying them by the psychic impressions left at crime scenes. Psychics have also been known to track down missing people, both alive and dead. Many techniques are used to contact supernatural entities, including hypnotism and drugs, which can be very dangerous. This sheer variety of methods is one reason why scientists have found it difficult to formulate theories about the alleged paranormal abilities of psychics and mediums.

AUTOMATIC WRITING

Writing without conscious control could be thought of as receiving messages from the spirit world. The subject enters a trance while holding a writing implement and watching the reflection of a candle in a mirror. The writing produced is usually disjointed and incomprehensible but is sometimes treated as if full of meaning. This is not generally regarded as a very credible spiritualist technique because the trance state can easily be faked.

 FOOD FOR THOUGHT

Channeling methods assume that spirits can be controlled or contacted by living people through the power of rituals. Whether they are trying to banish a spirit or asking it for help, people use special items, words, music, mental preparation, or some combination of these to open up a link between themselves and the spirit. The ritual may be intended to affect the spirit, strengthening or weakening its hold on the ordinary world. Or it may be designed to affect the person who is conducting it, raising their own spirit to a "higher plane." It's easier to judge whether something has worked on yourself than on another spirit.

CROSS MY PALM WITH SILVER

Commercial divination has been around for centuries but is most often perceived as connected to the Romany, or Gypsy, lifestyle. Traditionally, Romany blood bestows strong psychic powers on those who inherit it. Gypsies, who used to travel widely across Europe in caravans, were seen as accomplished fortunetellers. A crystal ball is often used by fortunetellers and mediums who claim they can divine the future by looking into its depths.

DIVINATION

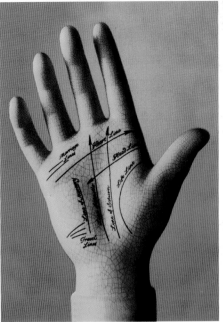

Divination means to foretell the future or, by magical, mystical, or supernatural means, to reveal what is hidden. Many of the divining methods that have been used for centuries are still in use today. Divination often involves a predefined set of symbols that can represent emotions, events, and personal qualities. By selecting these symbols, seemingly at random, and observing which ones occur in a particular pattern, fortunetellers make predictions about the future. Other forms of divination involve seeing visions of the future and making observations based on the physical qualities of an individual.

PALM READING

Palmistry, or chiromancy, is a form of divination that involves interpreting the lines on the palm of the hand. Unlike tarot, rune casting, and the *I Ching*, chiromantic predictions are based on an observed quality of an individual. Palmists associate each line on the hand with a different aspect of life. These definitions have developed gradually but are generally held to include the life line, the health line, the line of fortune, and the line of fate. Breaks and bends in the various lines signify important events in a person's life.

THE ZODIAC

The Ram, the Bull, the Heavenly Twins.
Next to the Crab, the Lion shines, the Virgin and the Scales.
The Scorpion, Archer, and He Goat,
The Man who carries the Watering Pot and the
Fish with the glittering tails.

This verse, "The Hunt of the Heavenly Host," helps us remember the 12 astrological symbols that make up the zodiac, a system used in several divining techniques. The positions of the planets, Sun, Moon, and signs of the zodiac at the time of a person's birth are believed to define his or her nature. The signs are divided into four groups associated with the elements: earth, fire, air, and water. For example, Leo, a fire sign, is associated with adventure and ambition.

FOOD FOR THOUGHT

Divination or guesswork? Accomplished fortunetellers can make educated guesses about the future of a client simply by assessing his or her appearance and personality. Predicting romance for a pretty girl or good fortune for someone who looks prosperous is almost certain to be accurate.

CASTING THE ORACLE

Divination often involves throwing down small objects and reading the patterns they make. Ancient practitioners described this method of divination as "casting the oracle." Originally, it was used for practical purposes rather than as entertainment, and the objects used were simple things that were easily found or made. Over the years, rituals developed around the various forms of divination, and the sets of cards, stones, and sticks used became increasingly elaborate and ornamental.

FORTUNETELLING WITH TEA LEAVES

Reading fortunes in tea leaves is not much in favor now that tea usually comes packaged in bags. Reading tea leaves is a simple form of divination. Once the tea in a cup has been drunk, the cup is turned counterclockwise three times. The patterns the leaves form are read to predict coming events. Romany Gypsies have an entire symbolic language with which to interpret the images. A padlock, for example, indicates that a door to success is about to open.

RUNE STONES

Casting rune stones is an ancient Scandinavian form of divination. The word *runa* means "mystery" in Anglo-Saxon. Rune masters were tribal magicians who used the power of their hidden language to affect the weather, harvest, healing, war, and love. The traditional Germanic set of runes uses an alphabet of three sets of eight runes beginning with the futhark. Later alphabets contain a blank rune to represent the unknowable. As with cards used in divination, the runes are drawn unseen and laid down in a pattern that allows their symbolic meanings to be applied to a particular question.

DOWSING FOR WATER

Dowsing is simply water divining, although some dowsers can also trace electrical cables, minerals, and oil. To the extent that it is no longer regarded as especially paranormal, dowsing has become accepted in the modern world. Traditionally, a forked stick is held out by a dowser as he or she walks through the countryside. If water is nearby, usually under the ground, the dowsing rod twitches. It has been suggested that dowsers are especially sensitive to Earth's magnetic field. However, some dowsers have found water by holding a pendulum over a map.

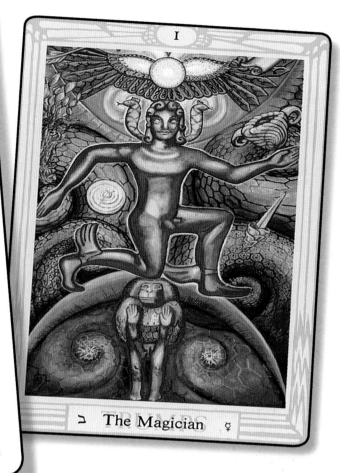

THE TAROT

The tarot is a special deck of cards used for divination. Instead of the four suits of hearts, spades, diamonds, and clubs in a deck of playing cards, a tarot deck uses suits of cups, swords, wands, and disks. Each suit has an additional court card. A tarot deck also contains 22 greater trumps known as the Major Arcana. All the cards have symbolic associations in addition to their apparent meanings. The different tarot decks offer different interpretations. The Magician, for example, can mean willpower or skill. During a tarot reading, the cards are laid face-down in certain positions to focus on different aspects of the subject's life. They are then turned over and interpreted.

FOOD FOR THOUGHT

Some divination methods, such as cartomancy and tea-leaf reading, involve the interpretation of random effects. Others study a quality of the person seeking information (the "querent"), as in palmistry or astrology. The difference between them is an important one. It is easier to believe that the querent's character might express itself through the lines on his or her palm, or might be influenced by the time of year of his or her birth, than that his or her presence can affect the fall of cards or twigs. It is also possible that the random methods of divination are used to give the diviner time to assess a person's character and to formulate an appropriate prediction.

THE I CHING

One of the oldest oracle books in the world, the Chinese *I Ching*, or *Book of Changes*, has lasted in its present form for at least 3,000 years. Divination based on the *I Ching* does not predict specific events. Instead, it shows possible outcomes of certain actions. It is composed of 64 hexagrams in different combinations of six broken or unbroken lines. Using random activities, such as drawing straws from a bundle or flipping a coin, a hexagram is produced and interpreted using the *I Ching*.

DREAMS & VISIONS

KUBLA KHAN'S PLEASURE DOME

In 1797, poet Samuel Taylor Coleridge composed 300 lines of poetry while in an opium-induced sleep. When he awoke, he could remember the poem and began to write it down, but after being interrupted by a visitor, he was unable to recall the rest of it. There are many instances of other writers, musicians, and artists gaining inspiration from their dreams. Parapsychologists have speculated that the sense of psi (paranormal sensory information) is not as strong as the senses of touch, taste, smell, hearing, and sight. Being weaker, it functions better when there are no distractions such as while a person is asleep.

Scientists are still investigating the processes of the unconscious mind. In his analysis of how the unconscious works, the forerunner of modern psychology, Sigmund Freud (1856–1939), paid special attention to the role of dreams. A Swiss psychologist, Carl Jung (1875–1961), later proposed that everyone shared a collective unconscious in which certain archetypal images recur, each with its own symbolism. Until the 1900s, there was no concerted study of the human psyche. Psychology (the study of the mind), like neuroscience (the study of the brain), is still a young science. Parapsychology (the study of psychic phenomena) draws on these other sciences, but there is still a lot to be discovered.

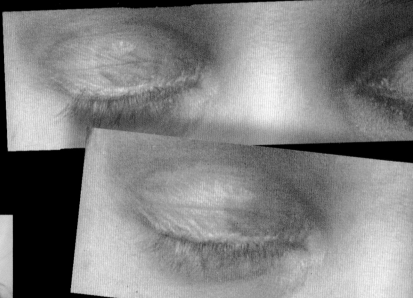

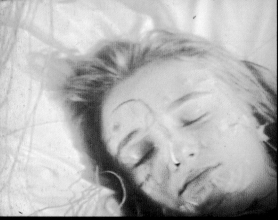

SLEEP RESEARCH

Studies conducted on sleeping people indicated they were more susceptible to receiving psychic messages while in the REM period of sleep. Experiments involved a psychic transmitting images to a sleeping psychic at different stages of a sleep cycle. Woken after each stage, the person could recall the images more successfully after REM sleep.

REM SLEEP

The mind is active and people dream during the rapid eye movement (REM) stages of deep sleep. The body goes through five sleep stages, from deep to light sleep. During deep sleep, the body repairs itself. People dream every time they sleep, although they might not remember their dreams. A technique known as lucid dreaming trains the sleeping mind to control the progress of dreams.

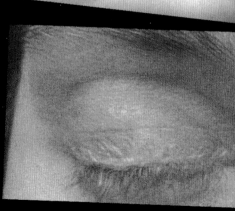

ANALYSIS OF DREAMS

There have been many theories about dreams. Ancient peoples believed they were messages from the gods. Freud, one of the first scientists who tried to explain dreaming, thought dreams were the wishes of the unconscious mind. More recently, Jung (right) wrote that in dreams people harness their creativity and come to terms with their fears. Modern sleep research tends to indicate that dreams are the result of the firing of neurons in the brain in order to help in the process of storing memories. Dreams are linked closely to the study of psychic phenomena because both are workings of the mind, which is only partly understood.

OUT-OF-BODY EXPERIENCES

Many people have reported having near-death or out-of-body experiences and commonly describe this as seeing a bright light pulling the soul away from the body. When the person is revived, he or she often reports having watched his or her own unconscious body being brought back to life. This "astral" body is claimed to be identical to the physical body but is transparent and shining. Ancient writings describe this phenomenon as a supernatural power that can be gained through magic or meditation. Skeptics prefer to put it down to hallucinations or delusions.

FOOD FOR THOUGHT

All these dream and vision phenomena can be attributed to the mind behaving oddly when it is on the edge of consciousness or beyond. Surrealist artists such as Salvador Dali deliberately induced this state in themselves. They believed it put them in touch with a higher level of reality and produced images intended to speak directly to their unconscious, perhaps drawing on universal symbols of a collective unconscious. Most people probably think they dream complex, strange, and interesting stories that would make wonderful movies or books. Dreams are never easy to write down when you've woken up, though!

EXPERIMENTS OF THE MIND

Parapsychology is the study of extraordinary mental phenomena, such as telepathy, that are experienced by human beings yet seem to have no physical cause. Many scientists are suspicious of parapsychology because it has become associated, wrongly, with other paranormal events such as alien abductions. Parapsychology research includes investigating extrasensory perception (ESP), which is the ability to receive information not available to the accepted five senses; psychokinesis (PK), which is the ability to alter the state of physical objects by mental activity alone; and out-of-body experiences. The study of parapsychology assumes that the potential of the human mind has been underestimated.

TELEPATHY

Paranormal research has recorded many instances of telepathy occurring in everyday life. Close family relationships, especially between twins, tend to increase the likelihood of telepathic connections. Some experiments in which the participants try to communicate over long distances have achieved impressive results. However, if ESP is some type of mental radio, it is proving very difficult to tune. Despite the high success rates, experiments have yet to prove the existence of viable telepathic communication.

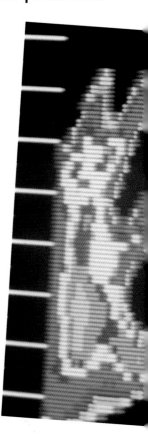

PHOTOGRAPHING AURAS

Many mediums have claimed they can see an aura of light around the human body. In 1939, a Russian engineer named Semyon Kirlian developed a diagnostic technique that could sense heat and electromagnetic fields. He photographed these auras using an electric coil, an aluminum plate, and photosensitive film covered by glass. His pictures showed people surrounded by a colored halo of light.

MILITARY APPLICATIONS OF PSI

Ever since the days when magic was used to protect the tribe, psychic phenomena have been investigated as a potential military aid. During the cold war (following World War II), the U.S. and Russian governments conducted serious studies of paranormal sensory information (psi) and how it could be used. For some years, a secret U.S. defense project at the Pentagon, known as Operation Stargate, has been rumored to be training psychics to use their abilities to see into enemy bases and to attempt to cause mental confusion in foreign military leaders.

JOSEPH RHINE

In 1927, Dr. Joseph Rhine and his wife, Louisa, started the first investigation into ESP at Duke University in North Carolina. This was the beginning of the science of parapsychology. Rhine invented the term *ESP* and spent 50 years researching the phenomenon. His work was first published in 1934. Scientists immediately found fault with his laboratory techniques and statistical analysis. Rhine successfully defended his techniques, but many thought his studies must have been experimental fraud.

ZENER CARDS

e of the earliest experiments in detecting psychic ability were Zener cards, a deck of 25 cards divided into five sets of five cards, with one of five different symbols on it. The cards were shuffled, and one at a time, a "sender" would try to telepathically project e symbol on each card to someone across the room. That person would attempt to "see" what card the sender was projecting. Rhine achieved a high success rate with this experiment under laboratory conditions. Some subjects were able to name the entire deck of cards correctly and others could predict in advance the order in which the cards would be shuffled.

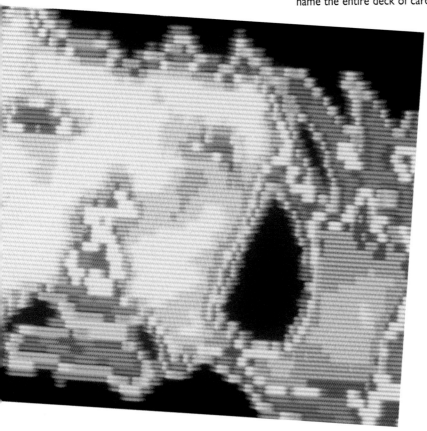

FOOD FOR THOUGHT

There is a one in five chance of correctly guessing which Zener symbol is being "sent." If an experiment uses 100 cards, the person "receiving" is likely to guess right 20 times. Anything significantly above that may indicate the existence of ESP. Parapsychology research has rarely been taken seriously by mainstream science because of doubts about the validity of the experiments. It is difficult to design an experiment that makes it impossible for anyone to accuse the researcher of faking results. In fact, some high-profile experiments have been faked or interpreted with a particular bias. There is always a possibility that if a researcher is convinced that the phenomenon is genuine, they'll read what they want to believe in the results.

MESMERIZING MINDS

Franz Mesmer (1734–1815) was an Austrian physician. He believed the human body has magnetic properties that could be used to cure illnesses. Mesmer undertook public healings that involved connecting people by cords to a tub of water filled with iron filings. He achieved some notable successes, but the scientific community remained unconvinced, and he was denounced as an impostor. Although Mesmer's work was largely discredited, it paved the way for the study of hypnotism and the unconscious mind.

KIRLIAN PHOTOGRAPHY

Some people who study paranormal events think that many of the so-called supernatural powers are natural to us. These may include the use of electrical and other energy fields. Semyon Kirlian's (see page 84) device could photograph the electrical and biogenetic energies transmitted by the human body. Although its use remains controversial, some doctors now use the technique to diagnose some cancers and psychological disorders. After death, a person's energies could perhaps leave behind a ghostly image.

A SHADOW OF OURSELVES

Another popular theory is that ghosts are human auras somehow trapped on this earthly plane long after the people have died. Apparently, each of us radiates an invisible electromagnetic energy field that, in the past, only people such as clairvoyants were able to detect. Modern science has confirmed that the human body emanates a field of energy that could be what has been described as an aura.

BEINGS FROM OTHER WORLDS

There are many similarities between the reported sightings of ghosts and those of aliens coming to Earth in unidentified flying objects (UFOs). Both are elusive, visible only at certain times and by particular people. Perhaps they are different aspects of the same phenomenon. "Aliens" may be manifestations of human spirits from Earth rather than from outer space.

THE LITTLE PEOPLE

Folklore is full of tales of mythical creatures such as fairies, elves, and dwarves. Although these "little people" are seen as purely fictional nowadays, it is possible that their origins can be traced to distant memories of creatures who did actually exist alongside humans. Perhaps they still do and remain mostly elusive, but when they are seen, we interpret their presence as ghostly.

PARALLEL WORLDS

Ghosts may not be the spirits of dead people from this world but are perhaps beings from a parallel world. They are not normally visible to our human senses, but occasionally, when conditions are right, we may catch a glimpse of them. The idea of other worlds existing undetected alongside our own is a very old one. Some people like to think the creatures of folklore and mythology are not simply the product of human imagination but are recalled memories of a past time when there was contact between our worlds. Parallels can be drawn to the animal kingdom in which creatures with a different range of senses to our own see an entirely different world than ours, even though we occupy the same space and time on Earth.

TIME TRAVEL

For centuries, humankind has been fascinated by the idea of the past, present, and future coexisting in parallel worlds, normally invisible to one another. Authors, such as H. G. Wells (1866–1946), and filmmakers have often used the idea. Although a controversial issue, physicist Albert Einstein (1879–1955) used his theory of relativity to prove that the existence of parallel time and space is possible. If it is, sightings of ghosts may be glimpses of people's past or future lives in another dimension.

CIRCLE OF HANDS

A long-established method of getting in touch with the spirit world is to conduct a séance. A group of people sit around a table in a quiet, darkened room. A medium, someone who is sensitive to the spirit world, acts as a go-between. Rituals are performed until the medium makes contact with a spirit and receives a message on behalf of one of the participants.

FOOD FOR THOUGHT

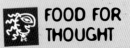

Various forms of telepathy may be possible between some people, especially if they are closely related. They may be able to communicate thoughts without actually speaking. Perhaps mediums can pick up thoughts and feelings about a dead friend or relative from participants at a séance. If so, they would, of course, be accurate. However, mediums may just be excellent judges of character who, over the years, have become expert at telling people what they want to hear.

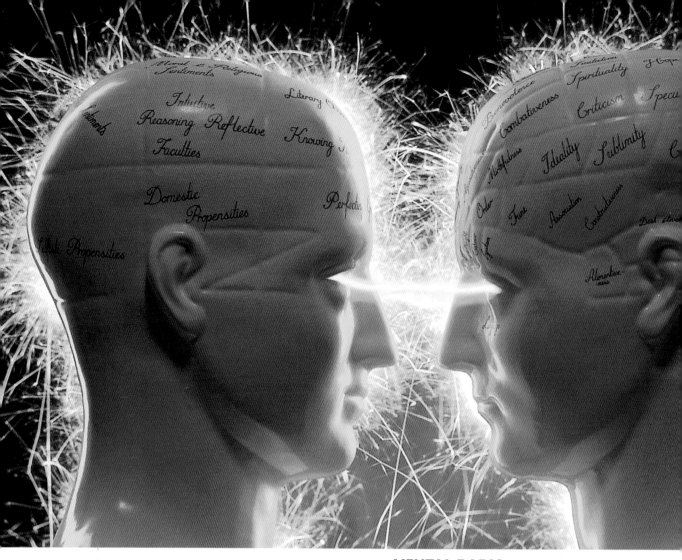

MENTAL RADIO

Recent paranormal research has attempted to understand what happens when successful telepathic communication takes place. It may be possible to observe brain activity during a psychic episode by recording the pattern of brain waves of an experimental subject. Some studies indicate that there may be changes in alpha waves, the essential carrier signals for the operation of the mind, when psychic abilities are being used.

BIOENERGETIC FORCE

In 1926, Russia was one of the first countries to conduct scientific research into psychic phenomena. Soviet scientists investigated the physical conditions necessary to enable the mind to transmit energy. In the 1970s, they did extensive studies of a Russian housewife named Nina Kulagina. Under controlled laboratory conditions, she was able to move objects, create burn marks, and increase the magnetic properties of objects without any physical contact with them. The force that Kulagina apparently possessed has been called bioenergetics.

ESP & PK

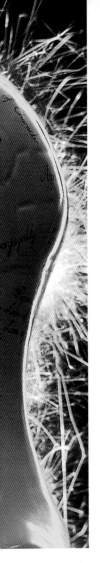

The two most widely researched areas of psychic phenomena are extrasensory perception (**ESP**) and psychokinesis (**PK**). **ESP** is generally held to include telepathy (direct mind-to-mind communication), precognition (having knowledge of unplanned future events), and clairvoyance (having a second sight, or the ability to foretell future events). **PK** is the movement of objects by the power of thought alone. **PK** may explain the existence of poltergeists, ghosts who cause apparently untouched objects to break or levitate. It has been suggested that a teenager in a highly charged mental response to emotional problems could cause spontaneous **PK**.

GANZFELD EXPERIMENTS

The ganzfeld (total field) experiment was designed by parapsychologists to counter claims of experimental error. To achieve a relaxed and receptive state, subjects were put into an environment free of all sensory influences from sight, sound, and touch. A sender then attempted to telepathically communicate a randomly selected image to the receptive person. The receiver reported aloud all their thoughts, images, feelings, and impulses. The ganzfeld experiment achieved a high success rate. More subjects successfully projected and received images than would be predicted by the theory of probability.

RANDOM NUMBERS—DEFINITE RESULTS

Since electronic and computer technology became widespread, parapsychologists have conducted a series of experiments on the relationships between mind, matter, and energy. One such experiment measures the human ability to influence a random element such as which number will be cast when a die is thrown. Random number generator (RNG) machines produce an electrical data stream that a test subject cannot modify by any physical means. Experiments established statistically that most humans *can* influence which numbers will come up randomly. The success rate seems higher at a full moon, a time when magnetism in the brain may be affected by Earth's magnetic field.

PSYCHOKINESIS

In the 1920s, Baron Albert von Schrenck-Notzing, an investigator of the paranormal, worked with Stanislava Tomczyk (right) and Willi Schneider to convince scientific observers and members of the English Society for Psychical Research that it was possible to levitate objects by no known physical means. Neither psychics nor Schrenck-Notzing were ever suspected of fraud.

ANCIENT UFOS

ALIEN FOOTPRINT

This fossilized hominid footprint from East Africa was made by an ordinary biped, yet the rock is 3.5 million years old! Some ufologists claim the print predates *Homo erectus* (prehistoric man) and that it was made by a visiting space man.

"**I**n the 30th year, in the fourth month, on the fifth day, by the river Chebar," wrote the prophet Ezekiel in the Bible, "I saw something that looked like burning coals of fire." Ezekiel described how he saw wheels gleaming like a jewel, "being as it were a wheel within a wheel." This could be a description of a gyroscope. Ezekiel interpreted his experience as a vision of God. Nowadays, ufologists would suggest it was one of the first recorded sightings of an unidentified flying object (UFO).

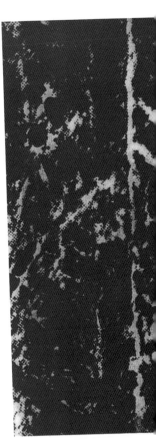

ANCIENT ABDUCTIONS

Celtic legends told of fairy beings who stole babies from their cribs and replaced them with fairy infants. To keep their babies safe, medieval peasants hung a knife over a cradle. Were these "fairies" alien scientists?

 FOOD FOR THOUGHT

Medieval thinker William of Ockham made famous a principle that, in today's language, amounts to: "Don't invent new theories when a simple common-sense answer already exists." Most of the evidence on this spread has a perfectly reasonable explanation, without postulating visits by space men.

PREHISTORIC RECORDS

These prehistoric rock drawings from Peru (above) seem to include astronauts wearing space helmets. Cave paintings sometimes show disks in the sky, and the Bible tells us that in prehistory "the sons of God" came down and took human wives. Could these be ancient references to visits by space men?

A DESERT MYSTERY

More than 1,000 years ago, in Nazca, Peru, thousands of stones were arranged to make vast lines and huge figures in the desert. The images, including the above "aliens," are clearly visible from the air but are difficult to distinguish while standing beside them. In 1969, writer Erich von Däniken suggested that "ancient astronauts" interfered with humankind's technology and genes and thus shaped human history. He claimed that these Nazca lines were made to be seen by alien visitors from their spaceships.

CULTURAL TRACKING

A Bible story tells of the prophet Elijah being carried away by a chariot of fire. In 1897, Americans saw airships, but in the 1950s, metal spaceships were seen (see pages 92–93). UFOs seem to appear in whatever form people expect to see them. This may account for the wide diversity of reported sightings.

FAMOUS SIGHTINGS IN HISTORY

c. 1450 B.C., EGYPT
Pharaoh Thutmose III sees "circles of fire" in the sky.

322 B.C., LEBANON
Shining silver shields fly over a city besieged by Alexander the Great. They destroy the walls by firing beams of light at the defenses.

A.D. 840, FRANCE
The archbishop of Lyon stops people from killing two creatures who had come to Earth in a "cloud ship."

1211, IRELAND
The people of Cloera try to catch creatures whose "airship" had landed on their church roof.

1271, JAPAN
The execution of a Buddhist monk is called off when a bright object hangs in the sky above the site.

1492
A sailor on Christopher Columbus's ship the Santa Maria sees a glittering object in the sky.

1639, BOSTON, MASSACHUSETTS
James Everell and friends are fishing when a bright light hovers over them and moves their boat upstream.

1752, SWEDEN
Farmers see a large shining cylinder in the sky "give birth" to smaller balls of light.

1762, SWITZERLAND
In different towns, two astronomers independently record a "spindle-shaped" aircraft move across the face of the Sun.

1819, MASSACHUSETTS
Professor Rufus Graves sees a fireball crash into the yard of his friend Erastus Dewey. They find wreckage and, inside it, a foul-smelling pulpy substance.

1820, UNITED STATES
Mormon leader Joseph Smith sees a UFO and speaks to its occupants.

1861, CHILE
Peasants see a metal bird with shining eyes and scraping scales.

1868, ENGLAND
Astronomers at Radcliffe Observatory, Oxford University, track a UFO for four minutes.

1887, BANJOS, SPAIN
Villagers find two "children" in a cave. Their clothes were strange, they spoke no known language, and their skin was green.

SIGHTINGS

UFOs undoubtedly exist. What *is* in doubt is what they are. Every year, more than 1,000 sightings are reported, many from people who ask to remain anonymous lest they be thought insane. Famous people who have seen UFOs include two American presidents; Jimmy Carter once watched a UFO while he was attending a dinner party and Ronald Reagan stunned a White House meeting by announcing that he had once seen a UFO from the window of his airplane. American astronaut Major Gordon Cooper reported seeing a glowing green object on his space flight in 1963—an object that also appeared on Australian radar. In 1965, space walkers Ed White and James McDivitt reported seeing a metallic UFO, with "arms" sticking out in all directions.

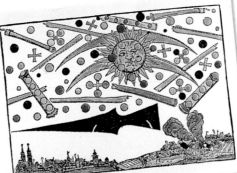

FOOD FOR THOUGHT

In the 1960s, the U.S. Air Force's Project Blue Book studied 13,000 UFO sightings. It found that only around two percent were truly unidentified. Most UFOs are perfectly natural phenomena. Explanations include:

- *Aircraft and satellites*
- *Weather balloons*
- *Jupiter (and other planets)—often unusually bright. A visual illusion called autokinesis can make them seem to move in the sky.*
- *Meteors*
- *Canadian scientists have found a correlation between UFO phenomena and earthquakes. Stress on rocks just before an earthquake can produce strong electrical fields and strange lights.*
- *Vitreous floaters (matter moving inside the eye itself)*
- *Wishful thinking, hysteria, and emotional disturbances*

Yes, it is less romantic! But even the UFO sightings not yet explained are also likely to be attributable either to natural phenomena that we don't yet fully understand (such as ball lightning) or to military experiments.

ALIEN WARFARE

This woodcut from 1561 (above) records a frightening event in Germany when black and red balls of light seemed to battle together in the sky. Some ufologists suggest that perhaps two alien species were fighting for control of Earth.

A UFO OF THE '90s

Jeremy Johnson, who took this photograph in England in 1992, at first thought that he had missed his chance, because the round white object vanished as soon as he pointed the camera at it.

THE AIRSHIP PHENOMENON

In 1897, many people in the U.S. saw shining, cigar-shaped "airships." This illustration was drawn for a newspaper at the time. Nobody would believe that they were seeing an actual airship, even though a certain E. J. Pennington said it belonged to him.

The Flying Saucer as I Saw it... by Kenneth Arnold

TUNGUSKA DISASTER

In 1908, an explosion in Siberia, Russia, flattened trees for miles around. No impact crater or meteor fragments were found, and modern theories of the cause include a comet or a small black hole. Local people, however, described an elliptical fireball that rose up from the ground. They subsequently experienced an illness resembling radiation sickness. Ufologists suggest the phenomenon was an exploding spaceship.

UFOLOGY IS BORN

Perhaps the most influential sighting of all was made by Kenneth Arnold in the United States. In June 1947, Arnold saw nine V-shaped UFOs. He told a newspaper reporter that they moved at speeds of more than 1,000 mph (1,600km/h), "like a saucer would if you skipped it across the water." The newspaper's subsequent report of "flying saucers" captured the public's imagination. *Fate* magazine was published one year later, the first of many UFO publications.

FOO FIGHTERS

During World War II, many British and American pilots reported seeing small shining disks (which they called "foo fighters") following their planes and causing the engines to short out. One ufologist thought these disks were remote-controlled alien probes. This World War II photograph shows these mysterious disks in the sky.

THE ROSWELL INCIDENT

This artist's reconstruction of the Roswell incident shows a UFO being struck by lightning in the storm of July 4, 1947.

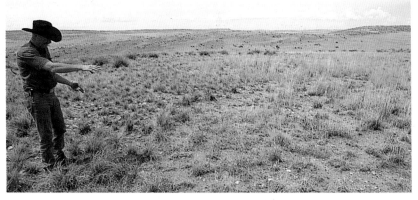

THE TRUTH IS OUT THERE

On July 8, local engineer Grady Barnett added to the Roswell mystery when he and a team of archaeologists claimed to have found a crashed disk-shaped UFO and the bodies of four aliens—small gray humanoids with large heads. The U.S. Air Force quickly removed these, leaving nothing to be seen. Even an investigation by the U.S. Senate in 1994 failed to convince UFO enthusiasts that their government does *not* still have the wreckage of a UFO and the corpses of aliens. The idea of a secret crashed UFO—and of what we might learn by "back engineering" such a machine—is so attractive that it is impossible to eradicate such beliefs.

THE MOST FAMOUS UFO

Leased Wire
Associated Press

Roswell Daily Record

RECORD PHONES
Business Office 2288
News Department
2287

RAAF Captures Flying Saucer On Ranch in Roswell Region

On July 4, 1947, there was a lightning storm over the town of Roswell, New Mexico. Sitting in his farmhouse, rancher William "Mac" Brazel thought he heard an explosion above the sound of the storm. The next day, riding out to check his sheep, Brazel discovered some wreckage "like nothing made on Earth." It crumpled like tinfoil but slowly straightened itself out again and was impervious to blows from a sledgehammer. Brazel reported it to the local air base, only to be arrested and held in custody until the wreckage had been retrieved. This was the prelude to one of the best known and most durable UFO stories.

CAPTURED!

Since the Arnold "flying saucer" story of June 1947, the U.S. Air Force had recorded almost 1,000 UFO sightings from all over the U.S., including reports of downed spacecraft. On July 8, 1947, the commander at the Roswell Air Force base told the press that a flying disk had been recovered from a local site. Immediately, according to the *Roswell Daily Record*, the Roswell wreckage became a crashed UFO from which four aliens had been retrieved.

ALIEN AUTOPSY

In 1996, businessman Ray Santilli released film, on authenticated 1947 film stock, of autopsies being done on the aliens retrieved from the Roswell crash. The movie was like a B-class horror film and the aliens looked nothing like those supposedly found in the Roswell crash. There was even a modern telephone visible clearly in the background. Yet UFO enthusiasts were convinced by the "evidence" of this movie. This picture, from the Roswell International UFO Museum, shows a replica of the alien body from the filmed "autopsy."

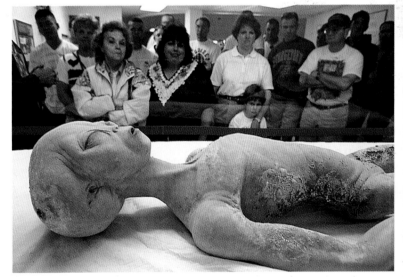

BALLOON WRECKAGE

On the afternoon of July 8, the U.S. Air Force held two press conferences. A polite, fresh-faced, and very plausible young warrant officer showed foil debris from a weather balloon that he said was the cause of the confusion. When asked if it was the remains of a flying saucer, the young man giggled. Was the government trying to cover something up? That same month, there were a number of U.S. Air Force cargo flights from Roswell to the top-secret Wright-Patterson Air Force base in Ohio. What they were carrying has never been satisfactorily explained.

FOOD FOR THOUGHT

After four years, the Hessdalen investigators concluded that the lights were probably a natural phenomenon. There is so much about our world that we do not understand that it is highly likely that UFO incidents are, in fact, natural but rare phenomena that we cannot yet explain. Only when we understand everything about our own world will we be able to say that inexplicable events may have been caused by aliens.

CLOSE ENCOUNTERS

During the 1950s and 1960s, there were thousands of **UFO** sightings, but it was not until 1972 that a way of analyzing and categorizing them was developed by J. Allen Hynek, a respected ufologist. In his book *The UFO Experience*, Dr. Hynek was the first ufologist to divide the different types of **UFO** events into types of close encounters. Ever since then, ufologists have classified **UFO** events according to his categories, from close encounters of the first kind to close encounters of the fifth kind. Many ufologists also give reports of these encounters a "strangeness" rating according to how typical of such events they are.

HESSDALEN LIGHTS

As well as photographing the lights, the researchers used radar, seismographs, infrared viewers, spectrum analysers, and Geiger counters to track and record evidence of their presence.

A CE2 PROJECT: HESSDALEN, NORWAY

During 1981–1985, Norwegian scientists studied lights that appeared over Hessdalen. The lights moved and seemed to respond to the actions of the observers.

CLOSE ENCOUNTERS OF THE THIRD KIND

Steven Spielberg's 1977 movie was based on ufologist J. Allen Hynek's book *The UFO Experience* (1972). In the story, a series of UFO encounters gradually builds up to a friendly meeting between aliens and humans (a CE5). It has been suggested that the U.S. government asked Steven Spielberg to make the movie to calm public fears about UFOs.

A CE1: THE LUBBOCK LIGHTS

In 1951, the people of Lubbock, Texas, reported a V-shaped formation of lights passing overhead at night. The lights were said to travel at around 400 mph (650km/h).

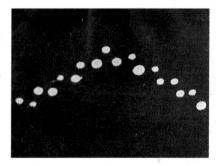

A nearby radar station also recorded an "unknown" object. Official explanations of the phenomenon include a flight of geese illuminated by streetlights and an experimental jet bomber being tested in the area.

CATTLE MUTILATIONS, CROP CIRCLES, & OTHER CE2s

CROP CIRCLES

In the 1980s, crop circles began to appear all over the world, especially in Great Britain and, as this example shows, Japan. Ufologists suggested they were made by landing spacecraft. Given celebrity status by newspapers, the circles received a great deal of publicity.

A close encounter of the second kind is when a UFO leaves some physical evidence of its presence. In one famous example in 1981, a French farmer from Trans-en-Provence reported that an object had landed in his garden. Government investigators found the soil had been heated to 1,112°F (600°C). One scientist suggested the effects had been produced by a strong electromagnetic field. The story is similar to that of another farmer, M. Masse, who in 1965 claimed that a spaceship had landed in his lavender field in Valensole—around 30 mi. (48km) from Trans-en-Provence.

A CE2 OF A DIFFERENT KIND

Stephen Michalak, an amateur geologist, claims to have seen a spaceship near Winnipeg, Canada, in 1967. Apparently, when the craft flew away, the heat was so intense that his clothes were set on fire. Later, the pattern of a grille appeared burned onto Michalak's chest. Some skeptics claimed that Michalak had burned himself, but scientists found evidence of radioactivity and extreme heat at the landing site.

CROP ART

One Australian suggested crop circles were caused by courting coots. A British expert blamed stampeding hedgehogs. But when a meteorologist said they were caused by stationary tornadoes, elaborate crop patterns started to appear that could not possibly have been made by the weather. This beautiful example appeared in Wiltshire, England. In 1991, two retired artists showed how they had faked many crop patterns in Great Britain. Strangely, many hoaxers have reported seeing UFOs while they were working on the crop patterns.

HOW DID SNIPPY DIE?

In 1967, a horse named Snippy (or Lady in some accounts) was found dead on a ranch in Colorado. Her head had been skinned with a straight cut and her internal organs had been removed. There was no blood on the ground and there were circular exhaust marks all around the body. Similar cases have been reported all over the world, notably a large number of horse mutilations in England in the 1980s.

 FOOD FOR THOUGHT

Why would aliens fly 2,000 light-years to play around in fields and why would such technologically sophisticated beings need thousands of animal organs for their studies? These stories are so unbelievable that no one would ever think they are the work of alien visitors. The real danger is that, swamped by the thousands of hoaxers and pranks, our scientists may miss the one witness who has had a genuine CE2.

CATTLE MUTILATION

There have been hundreds of reports of mutilations of cattle such as this example from New Mexico. Some people suggest they are the work of Satanists, but investigations of individual animals have shown that the blood in the flesh on both sides of the cuts has been cooked at a temperature of around 300°F (150°C), yet the cells around the incisions remained undamaged. Today, we know of no instruments capable of doing this.

Aboard a **Flying Saucer**

by TRUMAN BETHURUM

Non-Fiction—A True Account of Factual Experience

TRUMAN BETHURUM

Truman Bethurum was a road builder who, in 1954, claimed to have met aliens in the desert near Las Vegas, Nevada. His visitors had olive green skin and dark hair. They came from Clarion, a planet obscured from Earth by the Moon. Clarion, Bethurum was told, had no disease, crime, or politicians.

ABOARD A FLYING SAUCER

Bethurum claimed he had actually been taken aboard the alien spaceship, where he met the craft's captain, a beautiful alien named Aura Rhanes who spoke in rhyme. Bethurum met her romantically a number of times, much to the annoyance of his wife! Bethurum wrote a successful book about his experiences.

Flying Hav

Desm Geo

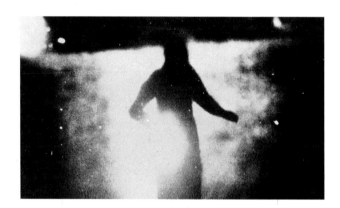

AN ALIEN IN NEW JERSEY, 1957

Born in 1922, Howard Menger said he first saw "space people" as a child and also had many close encounters while in the army. In his book *From Outer Space to You* (1959), he wrote about meeting Venusians, some more than 500 years old. They included a number of beautiful women in transparent ski suits—although the space woman in this photograph seems to be wearing a more conventional space suit. Menger claimed to have helped the Venusians fit into earthly society, cutting the men's long hair and offering the women bras! Menger said his second wife, Connie, was from Venus. In the 1960s, Menger claimed the Central Intelligence Agency (CIA) had asked him to make up the encounters so that they could test public reaction to UFO stories. He also said men in black (see page 104) tried to prevent him from talking about his sightings.

(see page 104)

🗨 FOOD FOR THOUGHT

All this evidence, like all UFO evidence, is merely anecdotal. It confirms ufology as no more than a pseudoscience based on unsubstantiated stories and hearsay. The stories are obviously ridiculous. Today, our interest in them is not whether they are true but why so many people in the 1950s were so easily taken in by these deceptions and what has changed in our society to make us less likely to believe such stories.

TAKE ME TO YOUR LEADER!

In a close encounter of the fifth kind, there is interaction between aliens and humans. The great age of the "contactee" was the 1950s, when many books were published on the subject and meetings with space beings were described by a number of speakers at public lectures. Nowadays, ufologists are embarrassed by these stories, which tend to discredit genuine UFO research.

JOE SIMONTON

Many other people claimed to have met space visitors. One strange case was that of 60-year-old chicken farmer Joe Simonton of Wisconsin. In 1961, he said he was visited by small, dark-skinned space men wearing black suits and ski masks. The aliens asked him for a pitcher of water and in return gave him some pancakes. Simonton ate one of the pancakes, which tasted like cardboard, and sent the others for analysis. They were made out of ordinary flour but with no salt. Local people said Simonton was a quiet, ordinary man who did not make up amazing stories.

FLYING SAUCERS HAVE LANDED

George Adamski was a waiter who later gave himself the title of *Professor*. He had written a novel about meeting a man from Venus but hadn't found a publisher. When he remodeled his story as fact, his book *Flying Saucers Have Landed* (1953) became a bestseller.

GEORGE ADAMSKI

In 1953, after seeing a UFO in the California desert, Adamski went to investigate. He met a handsome, suntanned young Venusian with long, sandy-colored hair who told him— using hand signs and telepathy—that Venus was Earth's sister planet. The Venusians had come to warn humanity that nuclear radiation could ruin Earth. Adamski later claimed to have been taken by his Venusian friends to Mars, Saturn, and Jupiter.

IS ANYBODY OUT THERE?

The universe is infinite. Even if life on Earth was created by chance, the universe is so big that somewhere in the vast expanse of space the circumstances that led to life on the planet could also have occurred elsewhere. Surely infinite space cannot be devoid of other life forms? Well, so argue science-fiction buffs and many ufologists. Out there, they say (as any *Star Trek* fan knows), there are hundreds of different races of every possible shape, size, and color. Or are there?

MARS FACE

The *Viking* expedition to Mars in 1976 photographed a rock formation, 2 mi. (3km) long, that looked like a face. Nearby was a collection of pyramid-shaped rocks. Ufologists claimed it was an ancient Egyptian-like civilization on the shores of a Martian sea. But in 1998, when Mars Global Surveyor rephotographed the area from a different angle, the "Mars face" looked like a meteor-battered mountain—exactly what it had always been.

BEYOND OUR DREAMS

Since the closest star to Earth is 24 trillion mi. (38 trillion km) away, SETI thinks it is "unlikely" that aliens have visited our planet. It prefers to see UFOs as paranormal phenomena. Even so, ufologists still find it difficult to believe that, in the infinite vastness of space, there is not life out there somewhere.

SETI

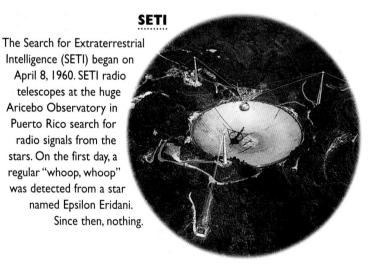

The Search for Extraterrestrial Intelligence (SETI) began on April 8, 1960. SETI radio telescopes at the huge Aricebo Observatory in Puerto Rico search for radio signals from the stars. On the first day, a regular "whoop, whoop" was detected from a star named Epsilon Eridani. Since then, nothing.

LIFE ON MARS

In Antarctica in 1984, a meteorite was discovered that matched the Martian rock studied by the 1976 *Viking* expedition. Scientists found organic molecules and tiny possible fossils. The excitement is not that life exists on Mars but that life can develop on other planets.

EXTRASOLAR PLANETS

This (right) is an artist's impression, but astronomers really have discovered planets in outer space. They use the displacements of a star's spectrum (the Doppler effect) to detect "wobbles" in its spinning. These betray the existence of another body in orbit around it. In October 1997, astronomers at a Swiss observatory discovered a planet circling the star 51 Pegasi. It is one half the size of Jupiter, orbits just 4.3 million mi. (7 million km) from its star in a "year" of only four days, and has a surface temperature of perhaps 2,372°F (1,300°C).

In November 1961, American radio astronomer Frank Drake (who later became the president of the SETI Institute) gave a lecture that changed our thinking about life in space. The answer, he said, is found in a mathematical equation:

$$N = R^* \times fp \times ne \times fl \times fi \times fc \times L$$

He explained that the number (N) of "space" civilizations is equal to the number of Earth-type stars in the Milky Way (R*), times the fraction of stars with planets (fp), times the number of those planets capable of supporting life (ne), times the fraction of planets on which life does, by chance, occur (fl), evolves intelligence (fi), and develops an advanced scientific civilization like ours (fc), times the number of years that the civilization survives (L). The problem with this equation is that we don't know the value of any of the factors in it. However, we can make some reasonable assumptions so that you can do the equation yourself.

1. In the Milky Way, there are around 25 billion stars roughly similar to our Sun (= R*).

2. Guess that one in five have planets (so R* x fp = 25 billion x $\frac{1}{5}$).

3. Guess that each of those stars has two planets like Earth (ne = 2), that life evolves on one in 100 (fl = $\frac{1}{100}$), intelligent life on one tenth of those (fi = $\frac{1}{10}$), and a scientific system comparable to ours on one tenth of those (fc = $\frac{1}{10}$).

4. Guess that each of those civilizations lasts 1,000 years, in a universe that has existed at least ten billion years, so L = one millionth (i.e., divide by one million).

Figure it out. How many Earthlike scientific civilizations are there in the Milky Way?

AREA 51

According to the U.S. government, Area 51 in Nevada does *not* exist—the area is blank on the map. In fact, it is a secret U.S. air base that may be used for testing prototype military aircraft, such as unmanned aerial vehicles (above right), or for dumping waste from nuclear weapons. UFO watchers regularly see craft performing aerial maneuvers there at night. They believe Area 51 is where the U.S. government has stored the Roswell UFO (see pages 94–95).

A SECRET TECHNOLOGY

According to Bob Lazar, the U.S. government has recovered some crashed UFOs and is "back engineering" its technology to see how they work.

MEN IN BLACK (MIB)

UFO witnesses have sometimes been followed by "men in black" who look like agents of the Federal Bureau of Investigation (FBI). Some UFO believers claim the MIB are aliens trying to suppress the truth. Or perhaps they *are* FBI agents. This MIB is from the Hollywood movie of the same name.

AREA 51: CONSPIRACY

"**D**on't be fooled!" say **UFO** enthusiasts. "Aliens do exist. The government knows about them and has worked with them for many years. But there is a cover-up to stop you from getting to know." To be a UFO believer, it is almost necessary to be a conspiracy believer. Conspiracy theories are immune to contradiction because they are beyond proof or disproof. No matter what a government does or says, the conspiracy believer shouts, "Trick!" Even when a claim is proved to be ridiculous or a hoax, conspiracy believers simply assert that they have been misinformed by the government in order to discredit them.

BOB LAZAR

According to Bob Lazar, who claims he once worked at Area 51, the U.S. government has nine UFOs stored there. Although there is no evidence that Lazar ever worked at Area 51, nor of his gaining an engineering degree from the college he claims to have attended, his testimony is often taken as proof that there is a conspiracy to cover up the truth.

MAJESTIC 12

In 1984, a TV company was sent some documents on photographic film. They seemed to prove that a group of experts called the Majestic 12 had been set up in 1947 to study the Roswell UFO. The fact that the documents had been typed on a typewriter not invented until 1963 was ignored, and conspiracy believers still think they prove that the U.S. government has a UFO. They say if the documents were faked, they were faked by the government in a conscious attempt at disinformation!

TOP SECRET
FOR YOUR EYES ONLY
THE WHITE HOUSE
WASHINGTON, D.C.

September 24, 1947

MEMORANDUM FOR THE SECRETARY OF DEFENSE

Dear Secretary Forrestal,

As per our recent conversation on this matter, you are hereby authorized to proceed with all due speed and caution upon your undertaking. Hereafter this matter shall be referred to only as Operation Majestic 12.

It continues to be my feeling that any future considerations relative to the ultimate disposition of this matter should rest solely with the Office of the President following appropriate discussions with yourself, Dr. Bush, and the Director of Central Intelligence.

Hary Truman

TOP SECRET
FOR YOUR EYES ONLY

🐦 FOOD FOR THOUGHT

American psychologist Elaine Showalter believes that conspiracy theories are deeply damaging to society because they poison our faith in our institutions. We used to believe we could always ask a police officer for help. Now, we feel that no matter who we elect, no government official or department can be trusted. Conspiracy believers have made the world a frightening and lonely place.

WHAT SHOULD I DO IF I MEET AN ALIEN?

NORDICS

This actor from the TV series *Alien Nation* illustrates another type—tall, Scandinavian-looking aliens from Sirius, Pleiades, or Venus. They are spiritual, gentle, love humans, and claim their ancestors were the first human beings—but watch out! Some of them have been captured by the Grays and fitted with implants to enslave them.

Many UFO enthusiasts believe that aliens are among us. One prankster on the Internet claims to have located 136 alien bases on Earth, with 14,619 aliens and a "robot army" of around 5,000 humans implanted with mind-controlling chips. Science fiction has imagined more and more sinister aliens in a variety of different forms. The sequence of *Alien* movies depicts beings that are impervious to human technology. They have acid for blood, no feelings or morality, and use humans as host incubators. The prospect of humankind ever being visited by such entities is terrifying. So what kind of aliens are you likely to encounter out in a forest on a dark and stormy night?

CHUPACABRAS (GOAT EATERS)

This group of aliens is said to live in the caves of Puerto Rico. Measuring a little over 3 ft. (1m) tall, they have huge red eyes, fangs, long claws, and vampire wings. They come out at night to mutilate, kill, and eat livestock. Some ufologists think they are the crew of a crashed spaceship, but they may be creatures that escaped into the jungle when a hurricane destroyed a secret government-research installation.

FOOD FOR THOUGHT

If you meet an alien, RUN! Modern UFO writers don't claim all aliens are dangerous, but there is enough evidence to convince you not to take the risk. SETI has sent radio messages into space. The 1977 Voyager space probe carried this message: "Greetings. We step out into the universe seeking only peaceful contact." They may as well have said, "Please come and eat us!" A common feature of abduction reports is that the aliens take small, meaningless things from humans. In one story, aliens stole a bunch of flowers from a woman. In another, they took fishing flies. So, if you can't run from the aliens, be sure to have some attractive trinket on you. It might distract them while you get away!

MIDGET MARTIANS

Like these midgets from the movie *The Man in the Moon*, aliens may be from a highly developed civilization, loving and lovable, and will usher in a world of health and happiness.

THE GRAYS

Grays are the aliens typical of most abduction stories, around 5 ft. (1.5m) tall with large heads and wraparound eyes. They come from Andromeda or Zeta Reticuli. Their military, totalitarian society aims to conquer Earth and make us their slaves. They have no feelings and conduct their medical and genetic experiments without anesthesia.

GREEN-SKINNED MONSTERS

Reports say that UFOs can "turn off" human technology and shoot down military planes. They have paralyzing beams and can abduct entire regiments of men. They do horrible experiments on people. If they exist, these beings are much more advanced than us, and they are dangerous.

FOOD FOR THOUGHT

One in six people needs psychiatric help at some time in their adult life. "Abduction" experiences are probably a form of mental delusion. The Hill and Walton cases (see pages 110-111) both illustrate the power of television to influence our subconscious minds. Even under hypnosis it is possible to tell lies, and there is considerable evidence that hypnotists can "suggest" UFO ideas to an abductee. In fact, experiments have been done in which subjects were able to invent realistic "imaginary abductions" under hypnosis. People have been observed having an abduction experience. In one case in Australia, two people watched as someone (who never left their sight) apparently "met" aliens and "went inside" a spaceship. It was clearly a real event inside the head of the "abductee," but all the two witnesses saw was the abductee's physical responses to what he seemed to be experiencing. Most abduction "memories" are similar. They involve tunnels, lights, being covered in liquid, finding it difficult to breathe, pain in the navel, being medically examined, etc. Female abductees remember having eggs taken from their ovaries, or even being implanted with alien fetuses. In these details, most "abductions" seem more like a flashback to the experience of being born rather than of an alien encounter.

ABDUCTION CASEBOOK

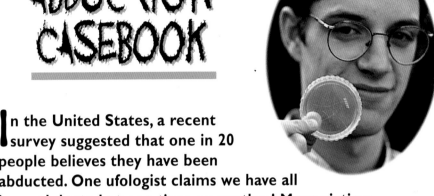

In the United States, a recent survey suggested that one in 20 people believes they have been abducted. One ufologist claims we have all been abducted at one time or another! Many victims realize they have been abducted only after their memories are drawn out by regression therapy (when a hypnotist takes them back to relive events in their past). A phenomenon that involves so many people is certainly worth investigating.

ALL OF THE FOLLOWING SYMPTOMS HAVE BEEN CONSIDERED EVIDENCE OF AN ABDUCTION:

- "Lost" time that cannot be accounted for
- Scars, bruises, or burns with no memory of what caused them
- Nightmares, especially about aliens, flying, or being eaten by animals with large eyes (such as owls)
- Insomnia, especially when caused by the fear of going to sleep
- Medical problems such as vomiting, headaches, fatigue, and rashes
- Depression
- A UFO sighting, experience of déjà vu, or a feeling of having second sight, the ability to foresee the future or see events happening elsewhere
- An image repeatedly coming to mind (perhaps put in the brain to block memory)
- Unaccountable black marks on an x-ray

IMPLANTS

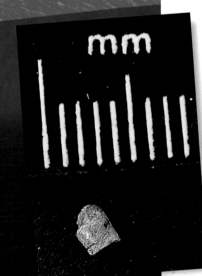

Some ufologists believe aliens implant tracking devices in the people they abduct so that they can locate them later. This implant was found in the roof of an abductee's mouth. Above, 17-year-old abductee James Basel with his alleged alien implant.

CASE STUDY 1: ANTONIO VILLAS BOAS, BRAZIL

Name/Occupation: Antonio Villas Boas. Farmer.

Date: Approx. October 16, 1957

Location: Francisco de Sales, Brazil

Case Description: The day after seeing a UFO, Villas Boas was alone on his tractor, plowing a field. Dragged onboard an egg-shaped craft by three humanoids, he was stripped, covered in a clear liquid, and had a blood sample taken from his chin.

Investigator's Notes: Villas Boas tried to fight off his abductors. Doctors found marks and scars all over his body. He suffered sickness and sleepiness that resembled radiation poisoning. Villas Boas remembered his experience without regression therapy and never changed his story. Boas remembered seeing some writing over the door of the UFO craft.

An artist's impression of one of Villa Boas's abductors and the alien craft that landed in his field

CASE STUDY 2: BETTY AND BARNEY HILL, U.S.

Name/Occupation: Betty (retired social worker) and Barney Hill (postal worker)

Date: September 19, 1961

Location: New Hampshire

Case Description: On their way home one evening, Betty and Barney were frightened by a UFO. They later found marks on their bodies and realized they had "lost" two hours. Nightmares and depression followed. Under regression hypnosis, they remembered being abducted by creatures with "wraparound" eyes. A needle had been inserted into Betty's navel. Betty remembered a "star map" the aliens had shown her and drew a copy of it. From this, ufologists deduced the aliens came from Zeta Reticuli, around 30 light-years from Earth.

Investigator's Notes: Although the Hills are often described as an "ordinary couple," Betty had had many psychic experiences. At one time, she claimed UFOs followed her everywhere. Her psychiatrist believed she was suffering from delusions after a frightening experience and that her husband had adopted her anxieties into his own memory. Their abduction happened shortly after a sci-fi program on TV had depicted aliens with "wraparound" eyes.

An artist's impression of Betty and Barney during their encounter with a UFO

CASE STUDY 3: TRAVIS WALTON, U.S.

Name/Occupation: Travis Walton. Logger.

Date: November 5, 1975

Location: Arizona

Case Description: One night in November 1975, seven men from a logging team saw a UFO. When Walton went to investigate, he was paralyzed by a beam of light from the craft. His friends fled, leaving him for dead. Five days later, Walton showed up in a nearby town. Under regression hypnosis, he remembered a typical abduction. He was examined by three tall aliens with large eyes and was shown a hangar full of UFOs.

Investigator's Notes: The Hills' abduction story had appeared on TV only one month before this incident. The team was behind on their logging contract and wanted an excuse. Travis Walton was known as a practical joker. But, 25 years later, not one of the seven-man team had changed his story.

Travis Walton wrote a book. His experience was made into a movie, Fire in the Sky, in which some of the facts were changed. Nonetheless, the team made a lot of money from their story.

CASE STUDY 4: LINDA NAPOLITANO, U.S.

Name/Occupation: Linda Napolitano. Housewife.

Date: November 30, 1989

Location: New York City

Case Description: In 1989, Linda Napolitano was having hypnosis therapy because she believed she had been abducted a number of times. During her treatment, she revealed she had been abducted again. Under hypnosis, Linda remembered being taken out through the walls of her 12th-story apartment into a spaceship high above the streets of Manhattan. She was medically examined and then returned to her bed.

Investigator's Notes: In 1991, this amazing story was given credence when two Manhattan police officers, who later claimed to be Secret Service men, reported that they had seen a woman floating in the sky and being taken into a UFO. Later, another witness also claimed to have seen the event.

An artist's impression of Linda Napolitano's abduction from her Manhattan apartment

FAKES

ROSWELL REVISITED

This effect, taken in Roswell, New Mexico, was achieved by photographing a UFOlike object thrown toward the setting sun.

U fology is a tempting field for con men who want to make money and publicity seekers who want to be famous. Some of the best work to expose fakes is done by responsible ufologists who know that fraudulent claims only add to public and government skepticism. The pictures on these pages show how some of the people can be fooled some of the time.

VENUSIAN SCOUT CRAFT

Special effects (FX) technology has improved so much that some past fakes now look ridiculous. This photograph of a "scout craft" taken by George Adamski (see page 101) looks no more sophisticated than a metal lampshade and some light bulbs. What Venusian would be brave enough to set off across the solar system in one of these?

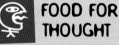 FOOD FOR THOUGHT

UFO photographers can't win, can they? Blurred blobs are rejected as too indistinct to show anything; brilliant images are dismissed as too good to be true. Nevertheless, after 100 years of UFO interest in the camera age, there is not one unquestioned, clear photograph of a UFO.

STRANGE CLOUDS, HAWAII

Photographed near Hawaii, this UFO is, in fact, a lenticular cloud formation, lit by the rays of the setting sun.

FAKE UFO?

Modern FX technology makes it more difficult to distinguish the fake from the real.
What is suspicious about this UFO shot?

ALPINE FAKE, ITALY

This UFO in the Bernina Alps is probably a tabletop model, photographed up close. The space-suited alien is almost certainly a toy soldier. It was exposed as a fake by the Italian Ufologico Nazionale.

HOW TO DETECT A FAKE PHOTOGRAPH

- Lack of adequate perspective reference that would indicate the size and position of an object suggests that the UFO is a model that has been hung up or thrown.
- Variations in the grain of a photo indicate that an image has been "pasted" onto it.
- Irregularities in the angles of light (and shadows) between the object and the background are evidence of separate images pasted together.
- Differences in color, clarity, or brightness between the UFO and the rest of the photo are often signs that the UFO has been painted or stuck onto a pane of glass in front of the camera.
- Bright luminous blobs or streaks may be blemishes on the film negative or lens flare and reflection. These account for many UFO pictures caught by accident.
- Things such as tree branches or telephone lines above a UFO indicate that an object might have been hung up close to the camera.
- Photographs conveniently blurred, fuzzy, or indistinct suggest a model that the photographer has tried to disguise.

SHARING THE MESSAGE

A constant theme of abduction stories is the "message to save humankind," usually a warning about the dangers of nuclear weapons or environmental pollution. Contactee Howard Menger claimed in the 1950s that space people gave him a model of the perpetual motion engine that powered their spacecraft, as well as some potatoes from the Moon. But why travel across the universe to tell us something we know already? And, having traveled trillions of miles, why give the message to Joe Nobody of Backwoodsville? Why not tell the president of a powerful nation?

GLOBAL CONQUEST

This is a favorite theme of sci-fi movies such as *Independence Day*. Some UFO enthusiasts genuinely believe there are aliens on Earth who are preparing for invasion and conquest by spreading new diseases and interfering with our weather. But if global conquest is their goal, why are aliens with the technology to cross the universe taking decades, even millennia, to take over Earth?

DESPERATE FOR DNA

Some UFO watchers think aliens are sterile or genetically mutated and are seeking to restore their health by splicing our DNA with their own. But why would aliens with the science to cross the universe need so many hundreds of abductees for their experiments?

WHY ARE THEY HERE?

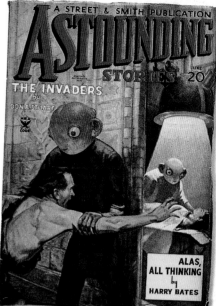

The main flaw in all accounts of alien visitors is how they got here. One respected ufologist thinks there are alien civilizations in the galaxy, but the closest is 2,000 light-years away. Traveling at the speed of light sounds feasible in science fiction. In reality, the technology to "fold space" or to reconstitute at its destination a being who has been "transported" seems impossible. For travelers at the speed of light, time comes to a standstill. In the time it takes to think *I must stop now*, they would travel an infinite distance in (for the rest of us) an infinite amount of time. They would end up beyond the universe at a time when everyone and everything was long since dead. And, given the difficulty of getting here, why would aliens want to visit Earth? What do we have that they could possibly want? Until we meet one who can tell us, theories abound. Some of them are shown on these pages.

SCIENTIFIC EXPERIMENTS

Some UFO enthusiasts believe that the human race is a huge genetic experiment. They think that because aliens have no emotions, they want to study concepts such as love, fear, and pain. This cover picture from a 1935 magazine shows that these ideas have a long history.

INTERGALACTIC TOURISM

The movie *Morons from Outer Space*, in which a group of extraterrestrial tourists (literally) bump into Earth, suggests another possible reason. Perhaps Earth is a galactic wildlife sanctuary run by aliens. Their rangers come to check that the human animals are healthy. Visitors are supposed to stay out of sight, but sometimes they become overinquisitive or accidentally turn off the invisibility button. And, of course, there is limited hunting!

FOOD FOR THOUGHT

The problem with all these theories is the discrepancy between the sophistication needed to cross the universe to reach Earth and the lack of progress the aliens make when they get here. Whether they come as scientific human watchers trying to stay hidden, conquerors trying to overwhelm us, or do-gooders with a message to impart, after 50 years they have all proved singularly incompetent in achieving their goals.

TIME SLIP

Occasionally, radio waves seem to "wobble" and listeners find their program interrupted briefly by a completely different channel. We imagine time as a knife edge rushing along, with a void before it and obliteration behind it. But if time were like a radio signal that can sometimes wobble, UFOs might be a random glimpse of the future. Time slip would also explain things like sightings of the Loch Ness monster, ghosts and the "walking dead," and disorienting experiences such as déjà vu, in which we have a sense of something having happened before.

THEORIES

Some ufologists think the popular definition of an alien as an extraterrestrial (ET) is misleading. Today, most ufologists accept it is unlikely that Earth is being visited from other galaxies. Instead, they prefer to define an alien as something outside normal human experience. Perhaps, some say, aliens are a spiritual manifestation. A 1950s contactee, Richard Miller, claimed an alien from Alpha Centauri told him that UFOs were angels. Other people believe UFOs are demons. The founder of the Aetherius Society, George King (a London taxi driver recruited by aliens in 1954 to help save the world from an intelligent meteor) claimed Jesus Christ was an alien from Venus. Other ufologists assert that UFO experiences are a real phenomenon but seek explanations that do not involve little green men in spaceships.

THE OZ FACTOR

Known as the Oz factor, a still and eerie quiet is often reported to occur just prior to an alien encounter. Ufologist Jenny Randles draws attention to the similarity between UFO events and paranormal phenomena such as extrasensory perception (ESP) and out-of-body and near-death experiences. She accepts the possibility of other beings in the universe but wonders if they are trying to get in touch on a psychic level.

ANOTHER DIMENSION

UFO experiences may be the result of our three-dimensional world coexisting with other worlds that have more or fewer dimensions. A creature living in a two-dimensional world would have no height, only length and breadth (like a sheet of paper). Such a creature would not be able to see up or down, as "up" and "down" would not exist in its two-dimensional world. It would be aware only of a very thin slice of the universe.

Now imagine if a ball were to pass through this creature's world. Until the ball broke through, the creature would be unaware of it altogether. Then it would see a mysterious circular shape appearing, growing in diameter, getting smaller again, and finally disappearing as the ball finished passing through.

If Earth shares space with and occasionally overlaps other-dimensional worlds, glimpses of these would be just as fleeting and puzzling for us.

WAKING DREAMS

These psychological experiences can be so vivid that in the dreamer's memory it may not be clear what was a dream and what was reality. Many waking dreams are disorienting, terrifying events. Later, to come to terms with the trauma, the brain might assign to it a symbolic but nevertheless concrete and explicable reality. In the past, people blamed ghosts or demons for their hallucinations, but today, because sci-fi images and sophisticated technology are familiar to us, our brain is likely to attribute these experiences to aliens.

FOOD FOR THOUGHT

These ideas are a retreat from ufology as scientific fact into UFO faith—where you can't prove but simply believe. In that sense, they demonstrate that no one has been able to prove that extraterrestrial spacecraft exist.

MODERN GHOSTS

I n these enlightened times of scientific reason and logic, we might assume that most supernatural matters would by now have been sufficiently well investigated for us to take a rational view of them. One certainly might expect the belief in ghosts to be on the wane, but it is not. There has probably never been more interest, and ghostly manifestations continue to be reported. While many of these may be hoaxes, there is a growing weight of evidence to suggest that ghosts *do* exist.

CAUGHT IN THE BEAM

In 1965, at Blue Bell Hill, in Kent, England, three young girls were tragically killed in a car accident. The ghost of one of them still wanders the stretch of road, and the local police station often receives reports from drivers who think they have knocked someone down. When they get out to investigate, they find no one there. Sometimes the girl hitches a ride and gets into a passing car but then disappears mysteriously. A similar story persists in Norway, where a sign has been erected on the roadside warning motorists not to pick up a ghostly hitchhiker.

MESSAGES FROM THE GRAVE

The answering machine of Jules and Maggie Harsch-Fischbach from Luxembourg is allegedly haunted and regularly receives complex messages from dead scientists. Research into the life force that seems to occupy some inanimate objects suggests that they could be haunted by a previous owner who has left a mental imprint on them psychokinetically.

FACES OF DEATH

In 1971, in the village of Bélmez in southern Spain, a ghostly human face suddenly imprinted itself on the pink floor tiles of a kitchen. When the family tried to rub off the troubled-looking face, its eyes opened wider and its expression saddened. The owner tore up the tiles and put down a concrete floor, but another more clearly defined face appeared. Experts in the paranormal were called in to investigate, and strange moaning sounds were recorded. Later, the house was found to be built above an old cemetery.

THE WHITE HOUSE

The White House in Washington, D.C., is haunted by a number of past U.S. presidents. Several ghosts are attributed to Abraham Lincoln, who was assassinated in 1865. His distinctive image has been seen by such notable personages as Queen Wilhelmina of the Netherlands while staying there, and by President Ronald Reagan's daughter during his incumbency. Lincoln himself believed in spiritualism and attended several séances at the White House, which may account for his powerful presence still being felt there today.

FOOD FOR THOUGHT

An often overlooked aspect of ghosts is the powerful effect that wishful thinking can have on the human mind. The power of positive thought is very real and is taken seriously by doctors and scientists. After the death of a famous and much-loved person, such as Elvis Presley, we long for them to live again. This sense of grief may be so strong that it could enable the human mind to externalize a familiar image that we then allow ourselves to believe is the ghost of the person we love.

DOES THE KING LIVE ON?

Elvis Presley (1935–1977) became one of the most idolized entertainers of his time. To many people, he remains the ultimate rock 'n' roll star. When he died in tragic circumstances, many of his devoted fans refused to accept it. Since 1977, he has supposedly been sighted in a variety of places worldwide, not just in the United States.

MODERN MONSTERS

Although we like to think we are less gullible than our ancestors, modern people find just as many things to scare them. But the monsters that scare us today are no longer dragons in the sea or goblins in the forests. We live in a scientific, technological age that creates its own monsters. The instinct to feel fear is part of our heritage. It may keep us awake at night and send shivers down our spine, but it also alerts us to look both ways when we cross the street and to stay away from dangerous animals and situations. Dragons, giants, and goblins may have disappeared inside storybooks, but that doesn't mean there is nothing to fear. In modern times, there are more monsters than ever before.

MINI MONSTERS

Just as our forebears feared the "little people," we have something tiny of our own to worry about. Our improved scientific understanding of what causes diseases has given us something very real to fear. We now know that under a microscope we can see scarier creatures than we could ever imagine—viruses, bacteria, and other tiny disease-carrying organisms. Even the ordinary head louse above looks monstrous.

FOOD FOR THOUGHT

Science can explain the dark and the animalistic, but it can't stop people being afraid. There will always be things we do not understand. Everything we learn uncovers another mystery, another monster, another scary story. Modern monsters are not borne out of superstition or religious beliefs but out of science and technology. We can see the tiny monsters that make us sick; we can imagine the terror of machinery gone crazy, a world poisoned, or a bomb to end all bombs. As long as there are stories to tell, there will be monsters to fear.

IRRATIONAL FEARS

Today, we are better educated and more worldly-wise than our ancestors, but that doesn't stop us from finding plenty to fear. Intense irrational fears are called phobias. There are many, including claustrophobia, a fear of enclosed spaces; acrophobia, a dread of heights; agoraphobia, a fear of open spaces; and arachnophobia, a fear of spiders. We know perfectly well that most spiders are harmless, yet many people are terrified of all of them. Some people are even afraid of moths. So it seems that monsters are still the products of our own minds.

THE ATOM

The atom is one of the tiniest building blocks of the universe, and the discovery that we could split it unleashed one of the most devastating weapons known to man. Nuclear weapons are now *the* most terrifyingly destructive monsters of the modern world.

ALIENS

Even though almost every inch of Earth has been mapped and millions of its creatures chronicled, some believe that there may be aliens out there somewhere—and if not already here, then on their way. Invasion and abduction by aliens are popular themes in science-fiction stories. It is almost as if we have a real need for an external enemy on whom to focus our fears.

RISE OF THE ROBOTS

Computers are taking over more and more of our lives. Robots help build cars and even perform surgical operations. But what if they go wrong? What if a computer bug makes a program work badly or a virus destroys it? Computers fly planes, run banks, and operate hospital equipment. What if the machines decided to run things without humans? It's a silly idea, but is it any sillier than the tale of a mountain gorilla or the idea that lightning could save somebody's life?

POLLUTION

In many ways, what we humans fear most is ourselves. As humankind uses more and more of Earth's resources, we worry that there will be nothing left for our descendants to enjoy. The more of us there are, the more things we manufacture and the more pollution we create. Perhaps we are the worst monsters of all.

PLACES OF POWER

LINES OF POWER

Ley lines are channels of power that supposedly run across Earth. Some people believe dowsers can harness these forces to help them find water or metals. It has been suggested that ley lines may have been constructed by primitive humans or an advanced ancient civilization, or are simply natural features of Earth. Large monuments or standing stones often indicate the presence of ley lines nearby. It has also been suggested that ley lines may be detected by variations in radio waves. In England, ley lines are believed to cross Glastonbury Tor (above), a place of great religious significance.

Despite all the research into the subject, psychic phenomena remain enigmas. We cannot say with any certainty whether or not they genuinely exist or how they function, but just like our ancestors, we are fascinated by psychic power and its potential uses. Over the centuries, the mystery of psychic phenomena has inspired many attempts to harness powers of the unknown. The legacy of those attempts is scattered across the world in the form of places of power. Some are natural sites in the landscape that are considered sacred. Others were built as a center for religious beliefs, magical practices, or primitive superstitions. These ancient places are thought to symbolize psychic forces that we do not yet understand.

MAGIC OF THE ANCIENTS

The pyramids of Giza are some of the oldest surviving human-made structures in the world. They were built before 2500 B.C. by Egyptian pharaohs to entomb their mummified bodies, along with the valuable possessions that accompanied them into the afterlife to signify how rich and powerful they were. From the dimensions of the Great Pyramid, modern mathematicians have figured out that ancient Egyptians knew the value of pi, the number of days Earth takes to circle the Sun, and the dates of important events in the future. Recently, it has been suggested that the position of the pyramids in relation to one another is identical to the layout of stars in the constellation Orion.

SACRED SITES OF THE ANCESTORS

Ayers Rock (Mount Uluru) in the Northern Territory of Australia is the largest single rock formation in the world and is a place of strong spiritual significance to the Aboriginal people. Many of the stories concerning Uluru are secret and are never repeated to outsiders. Around Uluru are many ancestral sites, and out of respect for Aboriginal beliefs, the Australian government has restricted tourist access to them.

STANDING STONES

Stonehenge in Great Britain was built around 1200 B.C., but we do not know for what purpose. It may have been an astronomical observatory, a Druid religious center, or a burial ground. In 1977, the Dragon Project was established to study electrical and magnetic forces around Stonehenge and similar monuments. There are many other standing-stone monuments in the world. Some of the most impressive are Carnac in Brittany, France; Msoura in Morocco; and Lake Turkana in Kenya.

FOOD FOR THOUGHT

Everyone feels a sense of awe and mystery when at one of these places of tremendous power. You don't have to share the beliefs of the people who built them, or those who use them today, to be amazed by the vision, dedication, effort, and genius that went into their construction. One of the most valuable things to remember about the power of the mind is that our ancestors, even if they had different beliefs to us, were just as intelligent and capable of achieving great things as we are.

WHY ARE WE SO INTERESTED?

In 1960, two French writers, Jacques Bergier and Louis Pauwels, published *The Morning of the Magicians*, a book that argued that science doesn't have all the answers. Society, they said, was like a car speeding along a highway—it was going somewhere, but what about the fields and villages on either side? By heading off down the science/technology road, they suggested, humankind was missing many of the important truths about life. The book revived interest in experiences that couldn't be scientifically explained. Perhaps part of the reason people are so interested in UFOs is that they are, and remain, a mystery, despite the many theories to explain them.

ESCAPISM

Prince Siddhartha Gautama (Buddha) lived in a palace and never saw the real world. One day, he went out and was so horrified by the suffering he saw that he left the palace forever. Today, we see the miseries of the world on television all the time. In a sense, we enjoy "going back into the palace"—getting away from reality and into a fantasy world.

FOOD FOR THOUGHT

Interest in UFOs and stories about alien encounters is probably here to stay. We are intrinsically fascinated by the unknown and the frightening. In a world where we are realizing that disliking other groups of human beings is wrong, perhaps we need the idea of some external threat such as sinister aliens—if only to play the "bad guys" in movies! Extraterrestrial UFOs can never be debunked, because science can prove only that something does exist, not that it doesn't.

THE MARTIANS ARE COMING!

In 1938, a radio adaptation of *The War of the Worlds*, a book by H. G. Wells, was so realistic that it created panic when broadcast in the U.S. Despite regular announcements that the play was fictional, William Dock, 76, from Grover's Mill, New Jersey (where Martians had supposedly landed), was ready with a shotgun to ward off the imaginary invaders. People almost seemed to want the story to be true.

THE WAR OF THE WORLDS

By H. G. WELLS

THE RISE OF SCI FI

Science fiction began in the 1800s, when it seemed that science would eventually be able to do anything. Readers found it fascinating, frightening, and exciting. Today, interest in science fiction is stronger than ever, and shows like *Star Trek* have huge cult followings.

THE SEARCH FOR SOMETHING BEYOND OURSELVES

The psychological need for "something out there" that is bigger than we are is as old as humankind. Today, fewer people go to church, but the need for something beyond themselves can lead to a belief in the occult or the paranormal. Interest in UFOs is perhaps part of this. One example is the Aetherius Society. Another is the *Urantia Book*, which was written in the 1930s by Dr. William S. Sadler, a psychiatrist and theologian. The *Urantia Book* teaches that the universe is full of many beings—gods, angels, and mortals (among which are human beings). It is not a religion, but people do attend study fellowships about it.

A SUBCONSCIOUS IMAGE

In his 1958 book *Flying Saucers: A Modern Myth*, the great psychologist Carl Jung called UFOs a "rumor." He said UFOs appeal to our subconscious—even their circular shape is a powerful subconscious image—and embody our deepest hopes and fears that science and technology will either save or destroy us. He concluded that to be fascinated by UFOs is a natural and inevitable function of our psychology.

INDEX